# A Passion for Colour

## Ruth Issett

SEARCH PRESS

First published in Great Britain 2013

Search Press Limited
Wellwood, North Farm Road,
Tunbridge Wells, Kent TN2 3DR

Text copyright © Ruth Issett 2013

Photographs by Gavin Sawyer at Roddy Paine
Photographic Studio
Photographs and design copyright
© Search Press Ltd 2013

ISBN: 978-1-84448-745-5

The Publishers and author can accept no
responsibility for any consequences arising
from the information, advice or instructions
given in this publication.

**Suppliers**
For details of suppliers, please visit the
Search Press website: www.searchpress.com.

Printed in China

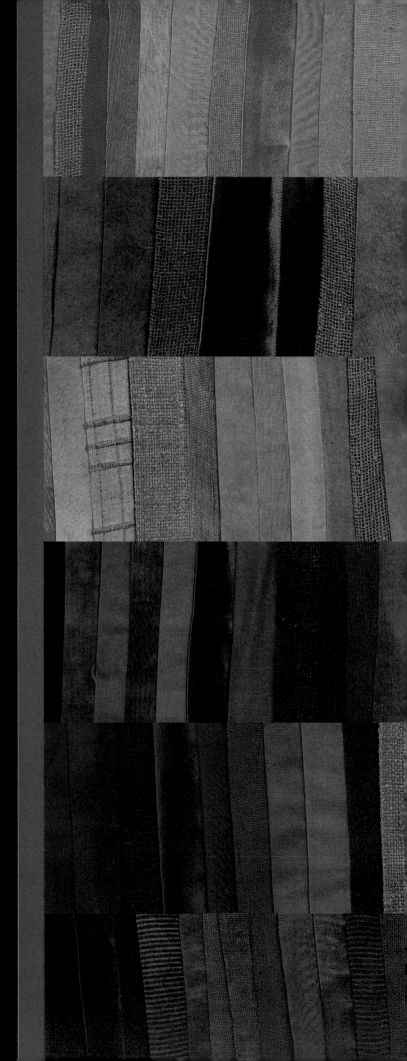

# Contents

# Introduction

I am passionate about colour. In fact, I am addicted to colour. It is definitely my comfort zone, although I realise that I still have a lot to learn about it. I am constantly aware of colour in my surroundings. I see it everywhere – in quiet moments as well as in hectic, busy times, and sometimes unexpectedly. Every day there is something to observe: the changing light caused by different weather patterns, the late winter sun just catching a small clump of trees or the reflection of a pink sunset on grey clouds. I don't tend to search out specific themes, subjects or ideas because colour can be found everywhere and in everything, and although most of my work is fairly abstracted, inevitably it reflects my personal observations of places and times.

When I am planning a course, preparing work or just relaxing in and around my home, I don't have to go very far to see colour and light. In the landscape around my home I can see colours that are sometimes subtle and at other times exciting and wild. Observing the different qualities of the light on the hills offers many choices. Sometimes the sky is dark and menacing but the sun lights up the undulating contours in vibrant acid greens. Occasionally rainbows connect silhouetted trees, while at other times the valley is filled with rich, autumnal foliage colours that contrast sharply with the recently harvested lush greens of the grassland. On a smaller scale, careful, detailed observation of objects such as leaves, stones or flowers can reveal fascinating colour combinations. Try to analyse what colours you can see around you and how they can be mixed or documented.

In writing this book, I have had to challenge myself to look at different colour combinations, and to try to understand why I select certain colours or techniques. Colours energise and excite me but can also bring a sense of peace and calm. When working in a lively, busy environment I will use strong, energising colours because those are what people are attracted to. When working in the relatively peaceful atmosphere of my own home, I might choose quieter, more subtle colour combinations.

## Light Moves
*A mixed-media painting using acrylic, ink and Markal Paintstiks on cotton-rag paper.*

I am fascinated by how colour responds to different surfaces such as papers, fabrics, threads and fibres, as well as printed and stitched surfaces. How I work tends to reflect the materials and media I use. I love the spontaneity of using wet media on papers and fabrics as well as the more thoughtful process of working with manipulation and layering or with the addition of stitch. I will often start with a comparatively speedy process such as dye-painting or printing, which can provide a great adrenaline rush. This might be followed by more considered additions: a drawn line, collaged paper or delicate touches of glorious stitch.

**Below, clockwise starting top left:**
*Blue and scarlet acrylic monoprint over-inked with scarlet, yellow and pink; green acrylic monoprint with a band of magenta and ultramarine ink, plus additional azo yellow Markal Paintstik; lemon, turquoise and white acrylic applied with a roller plus a small area of yellow monoprinting; yellow acrylic monoprint over-inked with turquoise, yellow and scarlet.*

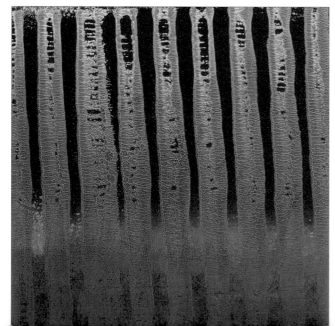

*Cobalt blue and titanium white Markal Paintstiks, applied and blended, then covered with magenta ink.*

*Controlled application of ink on to cotton-rag paper, using wet-on-wet and wet-on-dry techniques.*

There is excitement, maybe even fear, when you work with liquid media. Learning to limit or control the media is all-important, but in order to gain an understanding of this you need to be adventurous. You need to experience the excitement of the unknown, what might happen, and how one liquid responds to another and to a working surface. The unplanned element is key to this creative process; allowing certain things to occur and preventing other things from happening is all part of the excitement, and to achieve this you need to gain an understanding of the materials you are using. You can follow the colour wherever it may lead, or not. There are no rules as such but there are choices, and that is crucial. Spontaneity is important, but so is selection. It is all about the combination of accelerator and brake; too much 'acceleration' and things can get out of control, while too much of the 'brake' can hamper and restrict, leaving the work predictable and lacking excitement.

With the addition of stitch, drawn line or collage, more leisurely thought can be involved. The reflective process is less instant and can be more selective. There are opportunities to experiment with various colour options, exploring the layering and examining the possibilities of different surface qualities.

I am a practical person; I love to do things rather than just think about doing things. For this reason my journey with colour starts in a practical way with paints, dyes, inks, Markal Paintstiks, coloured pencils and pastels as well as resists and a variety of surfaces. Like so many people, I have a stash of fabrics and papers, and I love to explore the possibilities of using different media and surfaces. My mode of working may seem complex, and sometimes it is, but that is what makes it exciting and interesting as well as challenging. It is never boring, because there is always another aspect to be considered, a different combination to be tried or a new process to be investigated, practiced and possibly perfected.

# Yellows

lemons, limes, citrus, acid yellow, sherbet,
oilseed rape, buttercups, custard, yellow ochre,
mustard, sunshine, sunflowers, lichen, mosses,
clotted cream, daffodils, corn, wheat, sand,
saffron, canaries, turmeric

# Greens

emeralds, leaves, moss, spring, acid green, sage,
olives, grass, limes, aquamarine, viridian, slime,
leek leaves, sap, avocados, sea green, sea holly

# Oranges

tangerines, marigolds, ginger, sunsets, carrots,
hot coals, pumpkins, butternut squash, paprika,
auburn hair, fire

# Browns

sepia, burnt umber, burnt sienna, raw sienna, earth, tan, chocolate, mud, soil, terracotta, ochre, wood, moleskin, sable, coffee, tea, chestnuts, conkers, cinnamon

# Violets

mauve, purple, lilac, lavender, amethysts, gentian violets, aubergines, damsons, plums, blueberries, blackberries, blackcurrants, stormy skies

# Greys

storm clouds, stones, rocks, gunmetal, zinc, rain, mist, goose down, slate, granite, graphite, steel

# Blues

cornflowers, electric blues, icebergs, ultramarine, cobalt, cerulean, indigo, lapis lazuli, azure, sapphires, turquoise, aquamarine, jade, lavender blue, sky blue, powder blue

# Reds

brick, cherries, blood, wine, carmine, vermillion, scarlet, crimson, magenta, rose, peach, madder, alizarin crimson, cadmium, fire, turkey red, pinks, lipsticks, redcurrants, berries, candyfloss, Valentine's Day

# Materials and equipment

The materials that you use are important as they will affect the results that you achieve. It is worthwhile being selective in what you choose to work with. Of course, we all accumulate huge stashes of materials and equipment, and it is easy to be tempted by luscious, beautifully packaged items. However, it is important to experiment with the items you buy and not keep them untouched and unused.

The more I work, the more selective I become with the materials that I use. I like to work with fabrics, materials, papers and media that I feel confident with and which allow me to accomplish the ideas that are running through my head. I try to work with good-quality papers, chosen specifically for their characteristics and their receptive nature when using selected media. I use a comparatively limited range of fabrics and tend to buy natural or white fabrics in a variety of fibres, weights and weaves that colour easily with cold-water dyes. When it comes to choosing colour, I use a relatively limited palette. I work mainly with dyes, inks, acrylic and fabric-printing media. I have learnt to manipulate the ingredients, to manage the mixing of liquid colour, and thus have a rich palette to select from.

In this section I am going to suggest a comparatively limited range of materials and surfaces that I use extensively.

# Surfaces

## FABRICS

I prefer to use white or natural fabrics such as cottons, silks, hemp, jute and linen as well as viscose and rayon fibres plus mixtures. It is worthwhile looking for unusual plant fibres such as bamboo and banana. These will all dye well with cold-water dyes such as Procion MX, giving rich, vibrant colour. Think about the quality of the fabric you are considering: the surface texture, the density and how you might want to use it. Consider whether it is transparent, thin, fine, opaque, rough, smooth, shiny, piled, ribbed, heavy or dense.

The following fabrics are excellent to work with, especially for dyeing, sewing and various creative stitchery applications: **cotton fibre** – calico, muslin, sateen, organdie, cotton velvet, scrim; **silk fabrics** – silk chiffon, silk mousseline, silk georgette, noil, noil scrim, dupion, tussah, medium-weight habotai, organza, silk and cotton mixtures; **linen** – though not always easy to obtain, old linen sheets or tablecloths can be excellent candidates for dyeing; **viscose/ rayon** – viscose satin, silk viscose satin, silk viscose velvet, spun rayon, viscose chiffon, silk and viscose rib.

# PAPERS

Although I do have a small collection of unusual coloured papers, I tend to buy and collect mainly white or neutral papers that I can then ink, paint and print on. I love to spend time applying liquid colour to paper surfaces, observing how the colours respond to each other as well as how they mix and are absorbed into the different paper surfaces. These painted papers can then be cut, torn and collaged together to create visual ideas.

I sometimes prepare paper surfaces before I apply ink or acrylic print, for example by tearing, folding, crumpling, layering or with collage to create rough and smooth surfaces. Consider trying any of these methods for yourself. There are numerous types of paper all designed for different purposes such as drawing, wet work or pastel work. Cartridge and watercolour papers are readily available and come in different weights and finishes. Some of them are commercially produced, others are handmade. The more unusual papers are available from specialist suppliers, who should be able to identify the type and fibre content.

The following papers are worth trying and give a variety of different effects: white tissue paper, cartridge paper, watercolour paper, handmade cotton-rag paper, as well as the more unusual fibres such as lokta, which comes from Nepal, and kozo, a Japanese mulberry paper. Most papers are available in a wide variety of weights and types, and it is worth investigating them and trying some with inks and printing. Some will expand and absorb liquid colour, so some trials might be necessary.

*A small selection of the white and neutral papers I use. They include Japanese abaca, kozo and lace paper, Napalese lokta paper and artists' cotton-rag paper.*

I particularly like the handmade Indian cotton-rag papers as they are available in a variety of different weights and sizes with attractive deckle edges that can be used as a natural feature in your work. Lokta paper is another favourite. Available in a wide range of weights, it absorbs inks beautifully and becomes vibrant when dry. This paper is particularly strong once dry, especially when coated with acrylic wax or varnish. Kozo paper, which is also available in a range of weights, tends to be unsized and also absorbs inks easily. It is important to allow this paper to dry naturally, after which the colour will glow brilliantly from its surface. Kozo is an excellent choice for use in collage as it is soft, tears beautifully and is easy to glue in position. Also try abaca tissue and lens tissue. Both have an even, manufactured finish and are very lightweight but relatively strong. Abaca paper is slightly denser than lens tissue and will colour with ink beautifully.

*It is helpful to gather together a range of different weights of paper and colour them using a variety of different media, including inks, coloured varnishes, acrylic and wax resists as well as gluing and layering. I enjoy the process of mixing and applying the colour to the different paper surfaces, probably because it is similar to printing and dye-painting fabric.*

# Drawing and colouring media

When developing ideas and expressing things visually, it is important to work with materials that help you feel confident. Use a medium that you can control easily and gives the effect that you require. I tend to work with a comparatively limited collection of different media. Having used them for a long time, I understand them, and can adjust them to give the effects that I enjoy and require.

## ACRYLIC COLOUR

Acrylic colour is an essential part of my art-materials collection. I tend to use the slightly fluid acrylic colour as I like to print with it, but tube colour is also suitable. I usually select a very limited colour palette of lemon yellow, cadmium yellow, scarlet, magenta, turquoise or teal, ultramarine, white and occasionally black, from which I can mix numerous other colours. Working with a limited palette has allowed me to become familiar with the intensity, luminosity and subtlety of different combinations and mixtures. Acrylic colours can vary in their opacity, especially once white is added to them, and their transparency, opacity or translucency can be adjusted by the use of different acrylic gels and mediums.

*A selection of acrylic paints, which are available in tubs, jars, small bottles and tubes.*

## ACRYLIC GELS AND MEDIUMS

Acrylic gels and mediums have the ability to alter the quality and surface of not only acrylics but also all water-based colour. When confronted with these products, it is difficult to comprehend the sheer variety of applications and effects that can be achieved. When opening a container of acrylic gel or medium you will be confronted with a milky medium, either a solid gel or a liquid. Remember that a gel will thicken your acrylic colour and a medium will extend it and make it more fluid. Read the label on the jar or container to understand more about these acrylics.

Gels are available in soft, heavy or extra heavy, matt and gloss as well as various textural grades. They appear milky when wet, and they assume different qualities when mixed with colour and allowed to dry. A gloss gel will dry clear with a shiny surface, whereas a matt gel will be more translucent when dry with a matt surface. A soft gel will remain flexible when dry, and an extra-heavy gel can be applied fairly thickly and still dry clear.

Gels can have dye, lustre or bronze powders as well as other water-based colour added to them, and other gels are available that contain extra texture such as sand, pumice or granules, which can give interesting surface finishes. For more specific information about gels, the manufacturers' websites are full of helpful information.

Acrylic mediums will usually work in a similar way to acrylic gels, except they are more fluid. They dry quickly, so they are useful for layering or using as a resist on paper. Add dye powder to gloss varnish to make a coloured, shiny varnish, or add a lustre powder to an acrylic wax to give a subtle sheen. Try adding dye powder to a matt varnish to achieve a slightly milky staining on a surface, or applying gesso to give a layer of opacity or a slightly gritty (tooth) surface to your paper.

Sometimes when I collage different papers together, I treat the surfaces with some of these mediums to give added surface interest, resist and surprise. They are great fun to experiment with and give added depth and intrigue to work on paper surfaces.

## INKS

For years I have used Procion MX dye powder, a cold-water dye, as my ink when working on paper. I dissolve one teaspoonful of dye powder in 50ml (1¾fl oz) of warm water to make a rich colour and store the dye in a labelled, airtight bottle ready for use. I particularly like working with these inks as they provide a consistent colour palette when dyeing my fabrics.

*I love building layers of opaque, transparent and translucent colour to give additional depth and mystery to a piece of work.*

## DRY DRAWING MEDIA

I have a considerable range of different dry drawing media that I have accumulated over the years. All of the following are useful, and I suggest you build a collection of different types of pencil to make marks with.

Drawing pencils vary from hard (H) to soft (B). I prefer the B range of pencils for making bold and strong marks. I love graphite sticks, which are one hundred per cent graphite. They are chunky and are not encased in wood, so they can be used not just on their points but also horizontally for broad, strong marks.

Coloured pencils, water-soluble pencils and pastel pencils are all contained in wooden shells. I use coloured pencils to add extra, subtle detail to printed and painted surfaces, and to enrich an inked surface. When drawing with layers of different colours, some layers will obliterate others, while others will break up, giving a mottled surface. This means you need to think hard about which colour to apply first to get a specific effect. Some of the results can be surprising and unexpected.

I enjoy adding pastel pencil to my work. The chalky quality adds light-luminous colour to dark areas of inked paper, gradually bringing out the details. All pastels encourage you to be bold and messy, to build a surface of colour, perhaps working on a dark paper or a paper with a rough surface. Chalk pastels are pigment mixed with a gum; oil pastels comprise pigment mixed with oil and wax. Both are highly pigmented and therefore rich in colour, giving striking and bold effects. Oil pastels give a slightly sticky mark but can be applied with short, quick, repetitive movements, and they give intense surface colour. Chalk pastels are chalky, usually more delicate, but can be rubbed and drawn on to paper surfaces to give rich, bold colour. They need to be fixed with a spray fixative afterwards.

Markal Paintstiks are oil and wax chunky crayons. Rich in pigment and available in transparent, opaque and iridescent colours, they can be used on both paper and fabric. The colour can be smeared into paper surfaces or applied lightly to a textured surface. Being oil and wax they will resist water-based colour, which gives wonderful opportunities for resists and inked surfaces – very exciting, colourful and instant!

## FABRIC PAINTS

When working on fabric, I like to use a print medium that can be used for mono, block, roller or screen printing. There are numerous different fabric printing and painting colours available; some are very simple – you just open the bottle and apply them. Others involve mixing pigment colour with binders, which give the colour greater variety and flexibility. Procion MX dyes can also be thickened, giving transparent colour that is only suitable for plant-based and silk fabrics. When working on comparatively small areas of fabric I tend to use textile colour, which allows me to mirror my colour selection with acrylic colours. I can also adjust my print colours in relation to my dyed fabric, possibly adding a limited amount of opaque white. All fabric paints need heat fixing, either by setting with an iron or gently baking in a low oven.

## DYES

The use of dye is core to my practice. I nearly always paint my dye directly on to fabric and even undyed stitched surfaces. I love the way the liquid colour flows into a fabric surface. Every fabric, weave and fibre accepts the liquid dye differently, which is always exciting and challenging. Sometimes I mix my dye colours before brushing them on to the fabric; other times I might layer these colours, while wet, to change the colour gradually and subtly. I always rinse my fabric in cold water once the dye has been absorbed, making sure the excess dye and chemicals are removed. After allowing the fabric to dry naturally, it is wonderful to see the true nature and lustre of the fabric surface return.

Below: *A collection of drawing media, including Markal Paintstiks, oil pastels, chalk pastels, water-soluble coloured pencils, soft pastel pencils, drawing pencils and graphite pencils.*

# Threads

Over the years I have collected a selection of different dyed and coloured threads. Most of my stitching is applied either before a piece of work is dyed or afterwards to add emphatic colour at a later stage.

## NATURAL THREADS

I have a collection of medium-weight threads that I use for couching by machine or stitching by hand. These threads include cotton, silk, viscose cord and gimp as well as unusual knitting yarns such as bamboo, hemp, rayon and cotton mixtures. I select threads that are strong and smooth such as cotton perle for ease of stitching, couching and for whipped stitches.

## COLOURED THREADS

I prefer to hand stitch with medium-weight threads as I want the colour to be clearly visible, so I tend to select threads such as cotton perle, crochet cottons, corded silk and hand-wound silk, as well as my own hand-dyed threads. For machining, I tend to select strong cotton machine threads as I like to add clearly defined colour. I tend to use very simple machining, mainly straight stitching, occasionally couching thicker threads to the surface or working from the reverse with a thicker thread in my bobbin. I tend to use very simple techniques, making the result look more complex by the repeated use of different colours.

**Right:** *I colour-code my threads for hand stitching and machine couching and store them in transparent Perspex drawers so that I can see them clearly. They include cotton perle, stranded silk, crochet cotton as well as some knitting yarns.*

**Below:** *This luscious pile of threads is inspirational. It includes knitting and weaving yarns as well as hand-dyed yarns and embroidery threads collected over a number of years.*

# Equipment

Everyone needs some pieces of equipment if they want to create original works of art. It is easy to accumulate a wide range of tools, but eventually we all tend to limit ourselves to those we are most comfortable and familiar with and which allow us to create the effects we want with confidence and skill.

I use the following tools constantly and repeatedly. They suit my style, but that does not necessarily mean they will be right for you. One really useful item is a dishwasher cutlery basket that I store my tools in – it holds them neatly and vertically, and is easy to transport.

## PRINT ROLLERS AND BRAYERS

I prefer a medium-weight rubber roller that will move easily when mixing up acrylic or fabric paint. I endeavour to keep it very clean so that it will roll up colour effectively and evenly. I use a print roller to apply colour to print blocks, monoprinting surfaces and even directly on to paper and fabric. I love the way that colour can be mixed subtly, for example when shading from, say, yellow to blue through a range of greens.

**Right:** *Print on paper using both roller and monoprinting using scarlet, turquoise and white acrylic.*

**Below:** *A selection of useful equipment, including print rollers (brayers), shaper brushes, grouting tools, hand-cut print blocks, plastic canvas, palette knives, various bristle and synthetic paintbrushes as well as sponge brushes.*

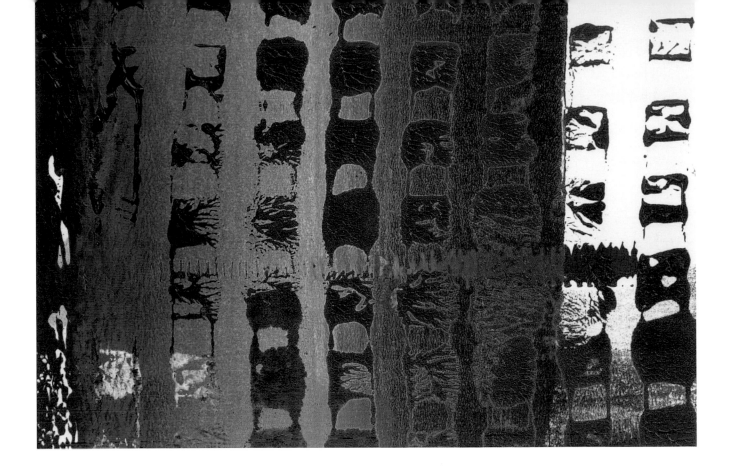

## BRUSHES AND MARK-MAKING TOOLS

It is useful to keep a selection of different monoprinting tools such as tile grouters, kebab sticks and wooden stirrers for quick pattern and mark making when monoprinting. I use a limited range of brushes, although I do possess a large number of flat wash brushes, from very fine-pointed to wide. I sometimes use a wide bristle brush to apply colour to a monoprinting surface, as it gives it a slight texture. A flat bristle brush is useful for applying colour evenly and for building a layered effect.

Synthetic watercolour brushes are excellent for applying colour to paper and fabric. They can be used to apply 'sticky' media such as acrylics and fabric paints as well as ink or fabric dyes. I have a few favourite brushes, particularly chisel-shaped flat ones as they can be used with the broad side or turned to give a fine, neat line. I have a small selection of these brushes in different widths and I always make sure I keep them clean by washing them thoroughly immediately after use.

Sponge brushes are invaluable. When applying large areas of liquid colour such as dye or ink, they are excellent for getting an even application. I tend to favour using a 2.5cm (1in) brush and I allocate one to each colour, thus avoiding colour dilution by regular rinsing.

Shaper brushes are ingenious, fine, rubber-tipped tools. They are available in a range of different points, widths and chisel-shaped tips and are very effective mark-making tools, especially for monoprinting. Comfortable to hold, they allow the user to draw confidently into acrylic or fabric paint.

## PALETTES

A deep, generous palette that will contain a reasonable quantity of liquid such as ink or dye is very useful. When dye-painting fabric, it is helpful to be able to soak the brush thoroughly in colour before applying it directly to an absorbent fabric surface. I use a selection of deep, radial palettes so that I have room for each dye colour and space in the middle in which to mix them together.

## PRINT BLOCKS

I like to create my own print blocks as it underlies the unique quality of my work. I use my large collection of blocks repeatedly and really enjoy them; for me, they are a form of drawing. There are now numerous print-block surfaces available that can be cut with simple lino-cutting tools. Even a large eraser can make a small, simple block. I also make print blocks using foam core board cut to a convenient size. I cover the surface with heavy-duty double-sided tape (carpet tape), to which I attach a variety of different objects including kebab sticks, tile spacers, washers, string or cut funky-foam shapes. Once positioned and attached to the tape, I give the block a very light coat of white acrylic paint, taking care not to get it too wet. The acrylic paint seals the surface and gives it a bit of tooth. Use wet wipes to clean your block as water will bow the foam core board.

# Sketchbooks

I firmly believe that it is important to have a sketchbook or even a number of sketchbooks. I have numerous different sketchbooks on the go at any one time and have kept every sketchbook I have ever used. I can therefore retrieve images, surfaces, colour combinations, ideas, trials and experiments quickly and whenever I need to. My sketchbooks provide a record of my work, and looking back through them is a fascinating exercise. I am amazed by how strong my style has always been, even if the themes have changed over the years.

Some people compile beautiful sketchbooks that are well-collated and beautifully illustrated, almost like published books, but do not be overwhelmed by these beautiful documents. Your sketchbook is personal to you and is simply a means of recording, playing and experimenting with different materials, equipment and techniques. The more you use your sketchbook, the more confident you will become – just remember that it is your book and you need to feel comfortable with it. Do not think that everything in the book needs to be beautifully drawn, neat and tidy. My sketchbooks are usually incredibly messy, not at all logical and all of different sizes and dimensions. None of them are works of art or even complete pieces in their own right, but they are my means of recording ideas and experiments, and exploring possibilities visually.

## What to buy

Sketchbooks vary in price depending on the quality of the paper, binding and covers, but are not necessarily very expensive. I love working in a large, spiral-bound book, building pages of colour and then working into the surface afterwards with print, inks and finally drawing to record how different media work. However, large sketchbooks are not always practical when travelling. They are heavy and unwieldy when working in a limited space or outdoors. I therefore have smaller spiral-bound sketchbooks, A4 (29.5 x 21cm; 11¾ x 8¼in) or A5 (21 x 14.75cm; 8¼ x 5¾in) in square, portrait and landscape formats, plus small A6 (14.75 x 10.5in; 5¾ x 4in) books that fit happily into a bag. I like the spiral binding as I can glue in additional pieces of work and bits of fabric without difficulty.

Hard-bound books of good-quality cartridge or watercolour paper are lovely to work in. Building up a collection that documents your progress, ideas and experiments in a bound book can provide a sense of achievement and permanence.

**Right:** *A selection of my sketchbooks, including spiral-bound watercolour paper and cartridge books, a bound lokta book, a bound coloured lokta book, and a much-travelled sketchbook full of collaged pages.*

# Using a sketchbook

I find keeping a number of sketchbooks invaluable. Some of my books have pages of drawings, done quickly to record a place or a particular colour combination. Others are collated to keep a particular body of work in order, for example an exploration of a particular theme or idea. I also use my sketchbooks as a means of documenting dyeing recipes, fabric samples and colour combinations, jotting down where I was when I did the work and the colours used. I have other sketchbooks in which I have experimented with different surface finishes for papers and printing. I have explored using gloss acrylic varnish for shiny layered colour; gesso to give ground and opacity. I have also experimented with different coloured pencils to give added drawn detail and colour highlights.

I work with a number of sketchbooks simultaneously: some are quite large, spiral-bound books that tend to be messy and well worked; others are smaller, spiral-bound books in which I document one or more series of experiments or ideas. I also use standard-bound books in which I draw and paint, especially when on holiday. I personally like the spiral-bound sketchbooks as I can open them flat, which helps when working with wet media. I sometimes glue in additional papers, which can make the book quite bulky. These large books tend to become quite messy but there is an energy and excitement on the pages. I do not consider them to be well organised but they are a working journal and an excellent way of recording ideas and trialling thoughts or processes.

I have some standard-bound books that have stout covers, containing different papers such as cotton-rag paper, watercolour and cartridge paper. I often take these on holiday with me, when I can relax and enjoy having the time to fill them with drawings, paintings and colour observations. When travelling I have to be selective with the media I take to work with. Sometimes I take water-soluble pencils and a paintbrush with a water reservoir. I like to work with inks and resists, so occasionally I take my dye powders too. I may also take a watercolour paintbox and have even been known to take a small bag of coloured papers and a pot of glue to do collage. Every situation has some limitations, but you just have to be inventive and not miss an opportunity to record what you see.

*A holiday sketch from the Summer Isles, Western Scotland, using water-soluble Inktense pencils plus some Procion MX dye, graphite and a white Markal Paintstik.*

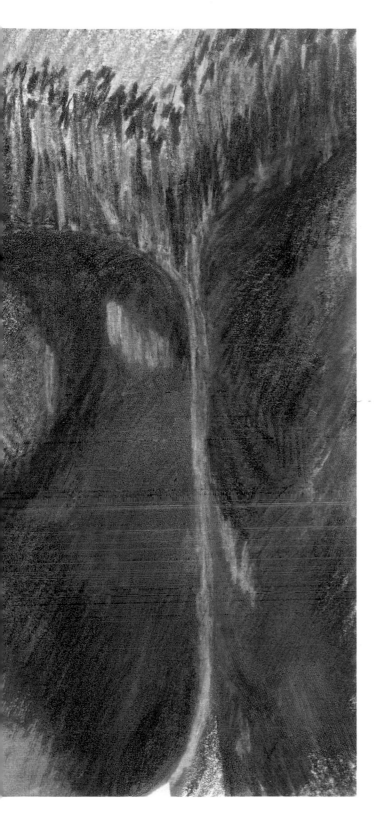

**Above:** *A water-soluble pencil drawing inspired by images of Western Australia.*

**Right:** *Drawing done on a hot summer afternoon in a French garden using coloured pencils and a little ink.*

A number of my spiral-bound books are used for recording processes. I have one book in which a series of different white or neutral papers are collaged together; some papers are glued, and some are just woven together. I have then added graphite to some of the pages, and white acrylic printing or black ink to others. I use these books to document samples created for demonstration purposes. At the end of a course I will glue these samples into the books as a record of a process or an extraordinary or unexpected outcome.

*A variety of different papers collaged on to a page of my sketchbook, then lightly painted with white acrylic. A limited area of black ink was added, then graphite pencil applied to emphasise the surface texture.*

I also have a set of square, spiral-bound books in which I keep the results of some simple colour experiments. They consist of a series of monoprints to which I have added colour in order to make them richer and more complex. I find these sketchbooks very useful for illustrating a particular process or idea quickly, particularly when teaching.

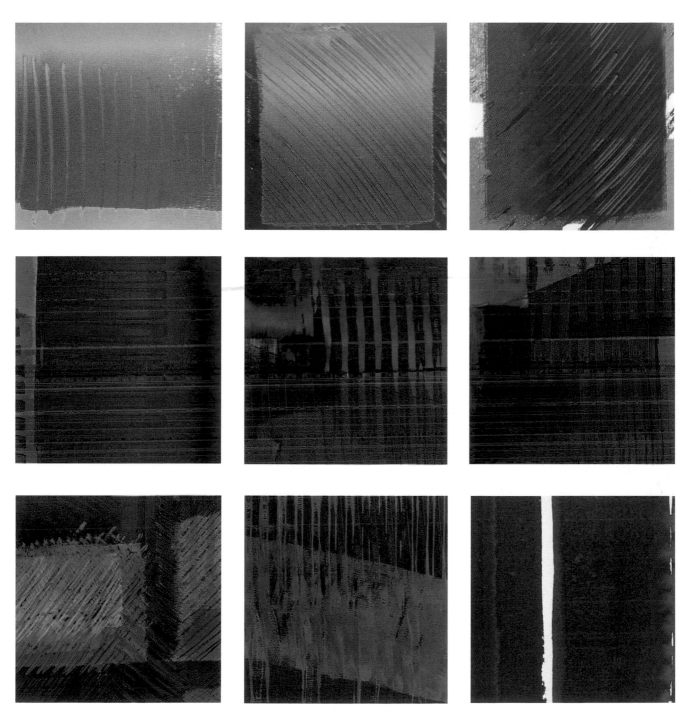

*Nine acrylic monoprinted squares exploring different colour combinations. The top row includes examples of the layering of violet and yellow, and the middle row shows red and yellow monoprints in layers with the further addition of pink ink. The two left-hand images in the bottom row are monoprints, initially using red and yellow with a final monoprinted layer of ultramarine and white. The last square uses Procion MX as an ink on cotton-rag paper, and explores the possibilities of controlling the ink as well as the effects of allowing it to bleed and mix on the paper.*

I also use sketchbooks to record dye colours, like a recipe book. I attach fabric samples with double-sided tape, showing what they look like before and after dyeing, with notes on the colours used, location and technique. These books are valuable as a record and as a reference.

2nd dip
using left over
colour

Blackcurrant

*Above: A double page from a small sketchbook used as a dyeing record. It shows a collection of silk, cotton and linen fabrics all dyed in a Procion MX dye called Blackcurrant.*

36

# Exploring colour

Colour is such a vast subject, and I often meet people who are nervous, intimidated and quite fearful of using colour. Working with just black and white might seem a simpler alternative: you choose either black or white. But what about grey? What about the proportion of black to white? Of course, black-and-white images are very striking, but by introducing greys and tonal areas they can also be very subtle.

My training in textile design has meant that I have had to use colour. I have explored different colour combinations as well as the effects of different fabric surfaces on colour, and over the years I have developed a passion for colour. I am fascinated by the effect of one colour on another, whether it is applied in liquid form through printing, inking or dyeing or by the placement of one coloured fabric or paper next to another. I like to be able to physically move colour, to adjust its position, to alter its tone, strength or surface. It takes time, in fact years, to build an understanding of colour, but the more you experiment the more combinations you will find that make you feel excited, energised and hungry for more.

**Below, left:** *Ultramarine, orange and white acrylic mixed and applied with a roller, and monoprinted.*

**Below, right:** *Mauve and white Markal Paintstik and ink on cotton-rag paper.*

**Opposite, clockwise from top right:** *yellow acrylic monoprint, inked with turquoise and with the addition of magenta-coloured varnish; layered monoprint using cadmium yellow and scarlet acrylic, with a further layer of ultramarine and titanium white applied with a brush and scratched with a kebab stick; layers of turquoise acrylic over-laid with a small area of scarlet-coloured varnish; collage using papers prepared with printing inks and Markal Paintstiks.*

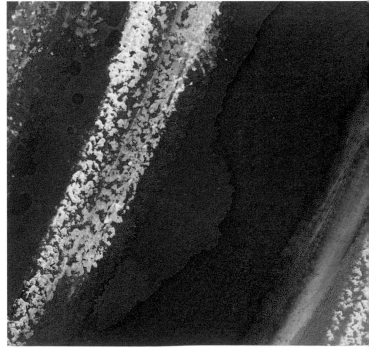

# Where to start?

First, make sure you are familiar with a good range of basic colours. Do not think that you can mix every colour easily just by using the three basic primary colours red, yellow and blue. By selecting, for example, a sharp, zesty lemon yellow; a warm, egg-yolky yellow; a strong tomato red; a rich, warm magenta; a deep, velvety ultramarine blue and a rich, azure turquoise, hundreds of colours can be mixed. To start with, choose colours that have varying intensities so that when mixed together the colour changes are clearly visible. Changes in darker colours tend to be less obvious, while changes in yellows are easily distinguishable. Select a black and a white too, as these can give you wonderful tints and shades – another area to explore!

So much can be learnt from mixing liquid colour and applying it to different surfaces. It can be great fun simply 'playing around', trying different colours and ending up with numerous new ones, but without discipline you will be unable to remember how you achieved them. By selecting a limited palette and being systematic in your approach, mixing can be both absorbing and fascinating, as well as giving you a useful record of the results of different mixes.

# Creating colour charts

There are various ways of exploring colour through colour mixing, and the more you experiment with them, the more confident with colour you will become. Take time to explore the potential of your favourite colours and broaden your understanding of them. Work methodically, and create some simple colour charts for yourself – they do not have to be neat and tidy! Use either acrylics or ink that will absorb well on to watercolour paper and, starting with a limited palette of lemon yellow, golden yellow, scarlet, magenta, ultramarine and turquoise, explore the different greens between yellow and blue, the range of oranges that can be mixed from yellow and red and the beautiful violet mixes of red and blue.

Through many years of working with acrylics and dyes on both paper and cloth, I have built a vast knowledge of how these mediums behave and how different colours are achieved, but there are still areas I have not yet fully explored and utilised on paper and fabric and in stitch.

## USING ACRYLIC PAINTS ON PAPER

Working with acrylic paints and using a print roller to mix the colour is a useful technique for exploring colour mixes. Acrylic paint is a slightly sticky medium and is relatively easy to control. By gently rolling it backwards and forwards and gradually introducing a second colour, wonderful, gradual colour changes can be created.

One method is to apply the acrylic paint to a strip of white paper, and gradually add the second colour in small, measured increments. The coloured strip is then folded into a concertina that can be stored easily and used for future reference. I tend to start with a lighter colour, say cadmium yellow, and very gradually add a tiny amount of a darker colour, such as magenta. Every time I mix a slightly different colour, I print it off on to the strip of white paper, creating a beautiful range of yellows, oranges and warm reds – a record of all the colours between cadmium yellow and magenta.

It is fascinating and very absorbing to vary the colours and see how the range of mixes changes. For example, mix cadmium yellow and scarlet and see how the oranges become harsher and sharper. Try mixing lemon yellow with turquoise, and lemon yellow with ultramarine. Then try cadmium yellow mixed with both of these blues to create totally different collections of greens.

When mixing ultramarine and cadmium yellow, the ultramarine will very quickly change the cadmium yellow to a murky green and then become very dark. It is difficult to distinguish the colours when they are wet but once dry a deep palette of dark greens and blues emerges, like shadows on a sunny day. Add white to these blues and greens to create a soft palette of greys, blues and greens, like fog, mist and clouds.

Other interesting mixes to try are ultramarine or turquoise with scarlet or cadmium red. Cadmium red is quite yellowy and therefore the mixes can appear slightly brown. However, by using very little red with the ultramarine or turquoise, the colour can remain bluish. This is most evident when adding white to it, producing a series of stormy violets and mauves that can be very attractive. Mixes of pure ultramarine and scarlet will appear very dark when wet and it is often difficult to distinguish colour changes as you mix them.

It is always worth mixing white with any of the above colour mixes. It helps to identify the strength and dominance of the component colours. By adding white to any colour, a whole series of tints can be created depending on the quantity of white added.

*A series of roller-printed acrylic strips, exploring the mixes of two different colours. From left to right: cadmium yellow and scarlet; scarlet and ultramarine; ultramarine and cadmium yellow; cadmium yellow and magenta; magenta, ultramarine and titanium white; and ultramarine, cadmium yellow and titanium white.*

# COLOUR MIXING ON FABRIC

Colour mixing can also be undertaken by painting dye directly on to a flat fabric surface. Try dye-painting a range of ten or twelve fabrics, each one a slightly different colour, working from one colour, say scarlet, through to, say, ultramarine. Start with the scarlet and gradually add small amounts of ultramarine, creating different reds, reddish mauves and aubergines. Paint half of the fabrics starting with scarlet and adding ultramarine, then paint the other half starting with ultramarine and adding scarlet, this time allowing the ultramarine to dominate. Remember that the colours will always look much darker when wet and before they are rinsed.

This is a quick way of creating a delicious palette of gently changing colours, and a collection of subtly related coloured fabrics is invaluable when designing and making textile pieces.

Always remember to add the darker colour to the lighter one – that way you will be able to distinguish the colour change. Occasionally, however, you may need to add a lighter colour to a darker colour. When adding turquoise to lemon yellow, for example, I find that I cannot achieve a true aquamarine. However, if I take a pure turquoise and add a tiny amount of lemon yellow, I obtain a wonderful aquamarine colour. All ink and dye colours have quite distinct personalities and characteristics – it is fun getting to know and understand them.

## Tip

You might decide to try mixing colour with inks (dye) on to paper first. Use a good, absorbent watercolour paper as this will absorb the colour easily. You can then progress quickly, distinguishing and observing the colour changes. By using dyes on paper, you can create a useful reference for selecting colours for fabric dyeing.

**Below:** *Scoured cotton and cotton organdie dye-painted with Procion MX, left: using mixes of scarlet and ultramarine dye; right: using mixes of turquoise and lemon yellow dye.*

## CREATING COLOUR SQUARES USING TORN PAPERS

Putting together a square of collaged coloured paper strips is really useful as it sharpens the eye, making you notice whether a colour is redder, bluer or yellower, lighter or darker, and why. Some people do this with printed coloured magazine papers or paint charts, but I prefer to use papers that I have painted with acrylic or ink mixtures myself.

Using a small square of white cartridge paper as a base, decide on a specific colour, say turquoise, and cut or tear as many small pieces of turquoise paper as possible. You will soon find that some are greener than others, some bluer, some paler and some darker. Now try to fit them together. Some may look very green, so try to arrange these on one side of the square and work towards the bluer ones. You could also try this exercise with yellows, blues or reds, then perhaps oranges, greens and violets. Make a brown square and see what happens to colours such as beige, taupe and coffee, or try black with various shades of grey.

# CREATING A COLOUR WHEEL

Another interesting way of creating a useful visual colour reference is
to arrange the coloured paper strips in a circle, like the one below. This
shows the primary colours – red, yellow and blue – with the corresponding
secondary colours – orange, green and violet – in between, and illustrates
the continuous and circular relationship between them.

# COMPLEMENTARY COLOURS

Complementary colours are pairs of colours that lie opposite each other on the colour wheel. Placed together, they create vibrant colour combinations, full of energy and excitement. Explore them by cutting windows into paper collage and backing them with complementary coloured blocks. Try violet blocks in yellow and vice versa and observe how the appearance of the violet varies. Each pair of complementary colours – red and green, orange and blue, yellow and violet – will have different visual qualities depending on where they are placed.

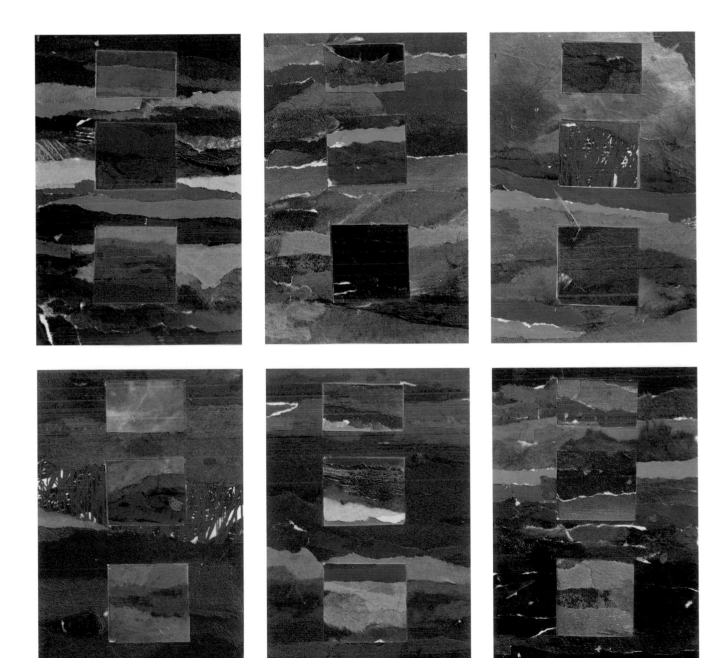

*Paper-collaged rectangles of blue, green, yellow, orange, red and violet with small areas of complementary colours behind cut windows.*

# CREATING COLOUR SQUARES USING FABRIC COLLAGE

Coloured fabric squares are fun to make and are excellent reference material. Take a series of similar-sized squares of white fabric and create fabric squares of colours using little scraps applied with small stab stitches or even bonded together. Rather than arranging the colours linearly, try to make the colours flow gently in all directions across the square, for example from lemon yellows to golden yellows, or from turquoise blue through medium blue, cobalt, denim and sapphire to ultramarine. Decide whether indigo fits into this square. Explore the possibilities of different oranges – those made with scarlet and lemon yellow compared with those mixed from magenta and golden yellow. Try to describe the sensation of different orange colours as they might appear in a bowl of tangerines, satsumas, clementines, kumquats, ruby grapefruit and oranges.

**Below and opposite:**
*I attached small squares of different-coloured fabrics from my collection to a lightweight backing. I then place squares of yellows, oranges, reds, violets, blues and greens within compositions or use them to trial differing proportions of colour within a piece of work.*

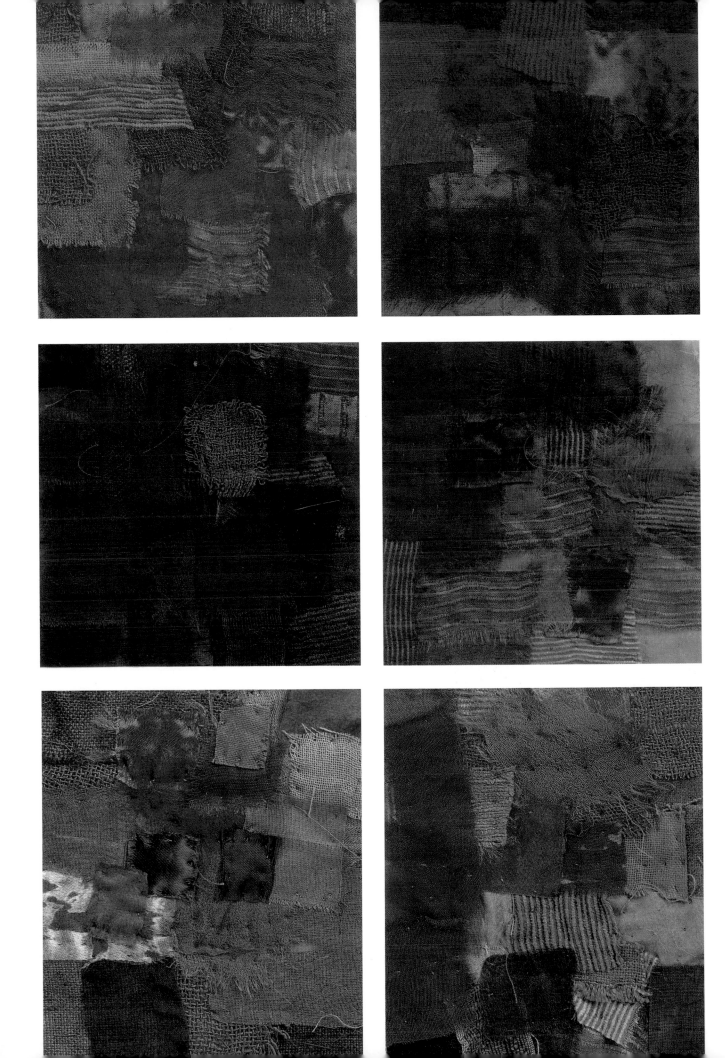

# Black and white

For many people, the blank white sheet of paper can be extremely daunting. Somehow that vast area of open space inhibits them, causing them to freeze up and become incapable of any relaxed or spontaneous movement. For others, the new page is liberating and exciting. They can't wait to get rid of the white sheet of paper; to get marks on to it and arrange them in some sort of design. I definitely fall into the latter category. I am not good at planning with a blank space in front of me; I prefer to arrange components within a space, for example loose pieces of paper to collage or liquid colour that has to be manoeuvred or manipulated into position.

   I enjoy the opportunity to collage together different white surfaces, either in paper or in fabric and stitch. By limiting yourself to the simplicity of creating with just white or near white, you become better attuned to texture and surface. Papers have different surface finishes – matt or shiny – and different textures – soft or brittle – and can be altered further by weaving, folding, crumpling, collaging, piercing, scratching and scoring. All these properties become even more important when dealing with plain white papers.

**Right:** *A collection of different silks, cottons, rayons and linens showing different weights and weaves.*

**Far right:** *A collection of different fabrics and threads with varying weaves and fibres, prepared for dyeing.*

**Below:** *Selections of white papers of various fibres and textures were glued on to a cotton-rag base. Papers were crumpled and folded before being glued down to vary the surface, then some were stitched with white thread.*

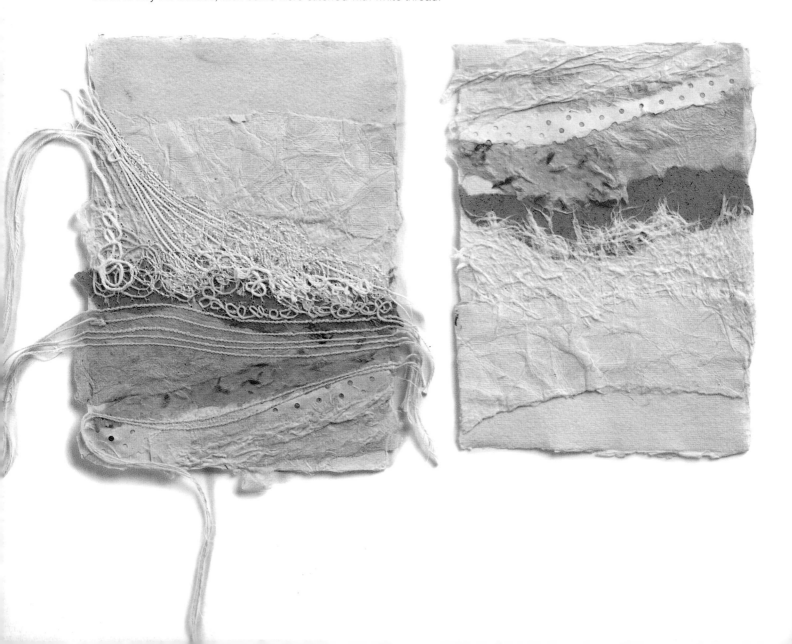

## WHITE OR NEUTRAL FABRICS

Fabrics can present further challenges and exciting possibilities. Because of their fibre content and their construction, fabrics can have a wide variety of different surfaces. A coarse, woven cotton fabric will have a slightly textured surface compared with a smooth, delicate silk satin. Fabrics can also have translucency and drape – characteristics less often found in papers. Layering white and neutral fabrics together will make you aware of their differing qualities and surfaces. This is invaluable information when you decide to colour them with either dye or print.

# BLACK

Black is a complete contrast to white; in its pure form, it is very dark and dominant. I can understand the attraction of working with black and white: the simplicity of the two extremes is powerful and demanding. By extending black, either by thinning with water or by smearing charcoal, pastel or graphite with your finger, you can quickly create tonal areas, giving depth and form. Gently add black ink to a dampened white paper collage, and subtle tonal areas can be created. Draw scratchy marks with a needle on paper to produce dynamic and forceful marks, especially when black ink is added. Manipulate, screw and fold a firm sheet of cartridge paper and then gently rub in graphite or black pastel – yet another exciting surface appears.

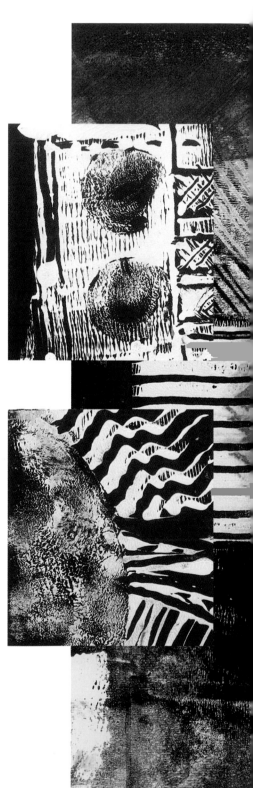

*Monoprinting was used to 'draw' on to a smooth black paper using white acrylic. The drawn marks were made with kebab sticks, shaper brushes and grouting tools and monoprinted from a polypropylene sheet on to the paper.*

I use very little black when mixing colour. I might use black adjacent to colour or in the background, but generally I find that it flattens colour. On the whole I achieve depth of colour or darker shades by using mixes of specific colours, though I do occasionally use black dye in conjunction with other colours as it has a blue quality that is useful for creating moody, muted mauves, plums and browns.

# Taking it further

To really understand the qualities, strengths and personalities of individual colours, it is important to spend time using liquid media, for example acrylic paint, ink (made from dye), fabric dye or fabric paint. Invest in a basic colour palette: for acrylic or fabric paint I would suggest lemon yellow, cadmium yellow, scarlet, magenta, ultramarine and a turquoise (either cyan or teal) as well as titanium white and perhaps black. For cold-water dyes (Procion MX) I would select lemon yellow, golden yellow, scarlet, magenta, ultramarine, turquoise and jet black. Of course there is no white dye, but tints can be achieved by diluting the dye colour. Spend time mixing these colours methodically in differing proportions and on different surfaces such as paper and fabrics, and you will discover an endless pool of colour. Remember to document your findings in sketchbooks.

Using dye on fabric is slightly more complex than using it on paper as the colour appears darker when wet than when fixed, rinsed and dried. However, the whole process of dyeing different fabrics, then processing them by rinsing, drying and ironing gives you an opportunity to study the colours closely and to become familiar with them.

*A collection of different cotton, silk, viscose and rayon fabrics dyed with a limited selection of Procion MX dyes. The intensity and quality of the colour relates to the fibre, its density and the type of weave.*

# DYE CHARTS

It is possible to create a useful reference chart by dyeing and over-dyeing fabrics. It is a lengthy and laborious process, but fun if you do it with friends, and fascinating when rinsing, drying and ironing the different-coloured fabrics and seeing the results.

When the fabrics are first immersed in the dye bath, the colours all look very similar. Once rinsed, variations start to appear but they are quite subtle; it is only when the fabrics are dried and ironed that the full range of colours emerges.

The first stage involves dip-dyeing one piece of cotton fabric in each of the following dye colours: Antique Gold, Golden Yellow, Lemon Yellow, Green, Turquoise, Ultramarine, Violet, Magenta, Scarlet, Orange, Rose Brown and Jet Black. I use Procion MX dye, and the fabrics are dip-dyed, fixed, rinsed, dried and then each subdivided into twelve equal sections.

The fabrics are then regrouped into bundles of twelve, each containing one piece of each coloured fabric. I place the fabrics in the same order in each bundle, with the colour I intend to use for over-dyeing at the front to aid identification after dyeing. The fabrics are held together tightly with a bead stitched at one corner.

Each bundle of fabrics is then over-dyed by placing it into one of the twelve dye colours, giving 144 different coloured fabrics altogether. Once over-dyed, the fabrics are rinsed thoroughly, dried and ironed.

At the end of this process you will have a dye chart like the one shown right – a useful record of the variety of colour that can be achieved when fabric is dyed in one colour and over-dyed in another. Each swatch of fabrics provides a wonderful palette of colours, showing the strengths and weaknesses of each mixture.

To achieve an even greater variety of colour, this process can be undertaken with a variety different fabrics simultaneously, for instance a cotton, a silk and a rayon fabric.

*Right: These fabric samples create a three-dimensional dye chart. The right-hand fabric sample in each row shows the first dye colour used. From top to bottom: Antique Gold, Golden Yellow, Lemon Yellow, Green, Turquoise, Ultramarine, Violet, Magenta, Scarlet, Orange, Rose Brown and Jet Black. All the fabric samples in each row have then been over-dyed using one colour from the same collection.*

# COLOUR MIXING

If you have spent time creating the colour charts on pages 43–45, you will already be familiar with colour mixing and the results you can achieve. You may even have noticed that some colours tend to dominate mixtures, bullying the weaker players. By exploring different colour mixes, you will very quickly become familiar with the characters of your favourite colours and obtain some wonderful results along the way. Explore lemon yellow with ultramarine when dye-painting, for example, and you will create some very naturalistic greens as well as a quite surprisingly acidic yellow-green, reminiscent of lichen or mosses. Other adjacent colours on the colour wheel, such as lemon yellow and turquoise, will also create lively, acidic, chemical greens, as well as aquamarines and emeralds. Magenta and ultramarine will produce strong, clear violets, purples, maroons and, when diluted with white or water, pale lilacs, mauves, pinks and cerise. Scarlet and golden yellow or cadmium yellow will give a range of rich reds and oranges. Add white to these and a range of peach, salmon, marigold and buttercup yellow can also be created.

Carefully adding turquoise to scarlet can create beautiful terracotta, ginger and brick colours. Adding white to this colour combination will reveal the strength of each component colour. Other combinations to explore are magenta and golden yellow or cadmium yellow.

When mixing complementary colours – yellows and violets, greens and reds, and blues and oranges (see page 45) – you are actually mixing the primary colours – red, yellow and blue – together in differing proportions. Ultimately you are likely to create a tertiary colour – usually some form of brown. This tertiary colour will be very rich in colour ingredients, with all three colours fighting for dominance, but by varying the proportions of the three colours in the mix, a wide and varied range of colours can be created. Add white to these colours and further subtle varieties can be unearthed.

**Above:** *A small concertina book created from pages of experimental roller- and monoprinting using turquoise, scarlet and white acrylic. As the acrylic colour was mixed and applied, a subtle mix of pale mauves, greys and pinks was achieved, which contrasts well with the strong, vibrant scarlet and the rich turquoise.*

**Left:** *A series of paper pieces using a combination of ultramarine and orange acrylic and inks. These colours were applied with a print roller, sponge brushes and simply monoprinted. Azo yellow and orange Markal Paintstik, with additional blender, were applied and then over-inked with ultramarine and orange inks, which have blended together to give deep brown-mauves.*

It is interesting to dye different plant-based fabrics (for example cotton, linen, viscose, jute and hemp) and silks together in a dye bath. Once dry, they will all be slightly different colours; different weave densities as well as fibre thicknesses will also affect the intensity of the colour achieved.

Each fabric shown here has been dye-painted using a mixture of just two colours. From left to right: silk organza dye-painted with golden yellow and additions of ultramarine; viscose satin dye-painted with orange mixed with dilute turquoise; silk rib dye-painted from lemon yellow to magenta; silk and viscose satin dye-painted with a dilute mixture of turquoise and orange; a cotton muslin dye-painted with golden yellow mixed with turquoise; and a coarse linen dye-painted with a mixture of scarlet and turquoise.

## ADDING TINY TOUCHES OF A THIRD COLOUR

Until now I have been describing the qualities of mixes using mainly two colours, but your understanding of colour can be developed further by adding in a third. For example, when creating a colour collection mixed from two colours and white, such as scarlet, ultramarine and white, try adding a small area of a third pure colour from the opposite side of the colour wheel such as cadmium yellow. Analyse whether this addition enhances, deepens or empathises with aspects of your original colour scheme. Another interesting experiment is to try adding a small amount of violet to a magenta and golden yellow colour scheme, or a tiny touch of light blue amongst red and orange.

It is important to remember that every time you have an idea, or the desire to explore a colour scheme or another technique, you will not always achieve what you hoped for. Along the way, though, you will become familiar with the processes, the equipment, the media and the surfaces on which you choose to work. It is important to remember not to be afraid to experiment. Record what you feel are successes and failures – sometimes failures might be considered successes when you revisit them later on. Try viewing the results of your endeavours from a distance or share them with others and observe their reaction – after all, the success or failure of a piece of work is highly subjective.

**Right, top:** *A series of prints was made using scarlet and ultramarine plus white acrylic. The prints used roller printing and monoprinting with different layers of colour. Finally, a touch of azo yellow Markal Paintstik was worked into limited areas.*

**Right, bottom:** *Orange and cobalt blue acrylic and white applied and mixed with a print roller. The colours are applied repeatedly in limited areas, sometimes over-printed with contrasting or adjacent colours as well as the addition of titanium white. Further areas of simple monoprinting were added using a mixture of these colours.*

**Below:** *Magenta and yellow plus white acrylic were rolled on to white cartridge paper. Additional areas of violet or golden yellow acrylic were printed on to these shaded areas. Finally, these prints were cut into rectangles and arranged into a horizontal composition.*

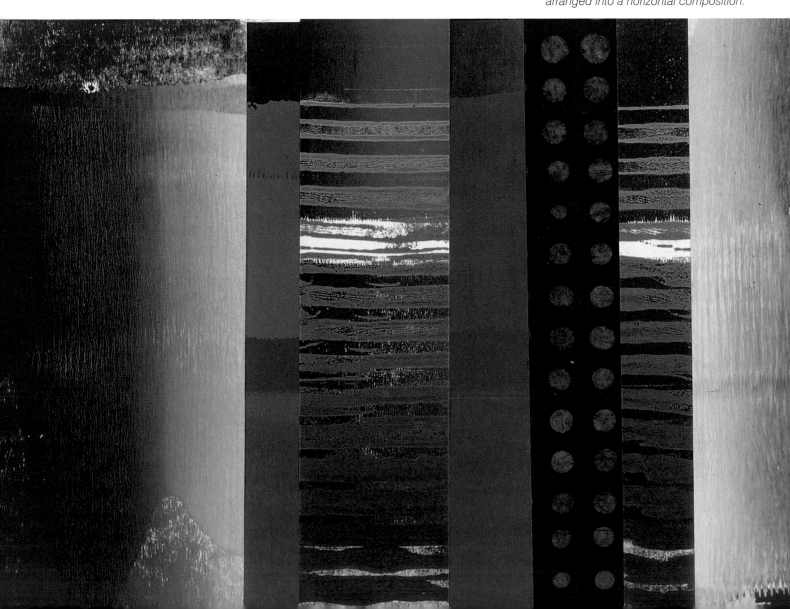

# Creating intensity, vibrancy and depth

I have realised over the years that the actual quality and finish of a colour and the surface to which it is applied will make an enormous difference to how the colour will appear. The contrast between a bright, shiny red and a strong pastel blue can be extremely intense – draw a pastel blue line over an area of bright scarlet and it is easy to see.

This presents another area of the colour to be explored – how the special qualities of the colour itself and the surface to which it is applied can be utilised. There are the various surface finishes of shiny, matt, rough and smooth, both in relation to paper and fabric. Colour itself has qualities of transparency, translucency and opacity, whether in relation to applied colour or different papers and fabrics. The repeated use of these qualities can considerably enrich and enhance the power of a colour and increase its depth.

**Left and right:** *Layers of transparent and translucent fabrics layered and stitched together with a small area of white printing. All the fabrics were stitched together in white and then dyed. This sample shows how different fibres and weaves absorb colour and how rich a fabric surface can become.*

# Transparency

Most paint and fabric colours are transparent. In other words, they are affected by the colour of the surface they are placed on. This is seen when printing on to a coloured fabric or a darker surface. Print a clear yellow on to a blue fabric and it will appear green; a transparent yellow on a red fabric will be barely visible. It is important to evaluate the depth or strength of the base colour and consider how the second colour will appear when printed.

The transparent liquid colour of inks can be layered repeatedly to give glowing colour. Watercolour paint is a popular transparent media, often used in subtle layers, building from the lightest colour to the darkest.

*Selection of papers inked, layered and varnished, with additions of Markal Paintstiks used as a resist.*

I sometimes use acrylic gloss varnish to act as a resist on paper and to give transparent layers of colour. Add a small amount of dye powder to this varnish and you can make a coloured varnish. Again, layering these coloured varnishes, working from light to dark, can give depth and richness of colour to a surface. Working on a white paper, apply a coat of yellow varnish, allow it to dry and then paint a layer of scarlet, slightly overlapping the colours. This, of course, will give a range of transparent yellows, oranges and reds. Alternatively, start from yellow and overlay it with turquoise varnish to achieve greens as well as aquamarines. The more layers you apply, the richer and darker these colours become.

These coloured varnishes can enrich acrylic printed colour. By layering transparent yellow varnish over an opaque, pale blue acrylic area, subtle layers of yellows, greens and greenish blues can be achieved. This all gives intrigue and depth to a piece of work. Some papers are particularly receptive to additions of varnish, especially if layered and repeatedly coloured. White papers such as cotton-rag paper and cartridge paper are comparatively smooth and varnishes can be applied to give a rich, glossy sheen. Applying coloured varnishes to a lighter-weight paper such as lokta will result in a strong, flexible, shiny paper that can be manipulated and applied to different surfaces.

Transparent coloured fabric is a different challenge. Certain fabrics are particularly transparent, such as silk organza, silk crepeline, synthetic chiffon and silk chiffon, but layered together the colours can be enriched and given deeper tones.

**Right:** *Dyed silk organza, illustrating its transparent quality.*

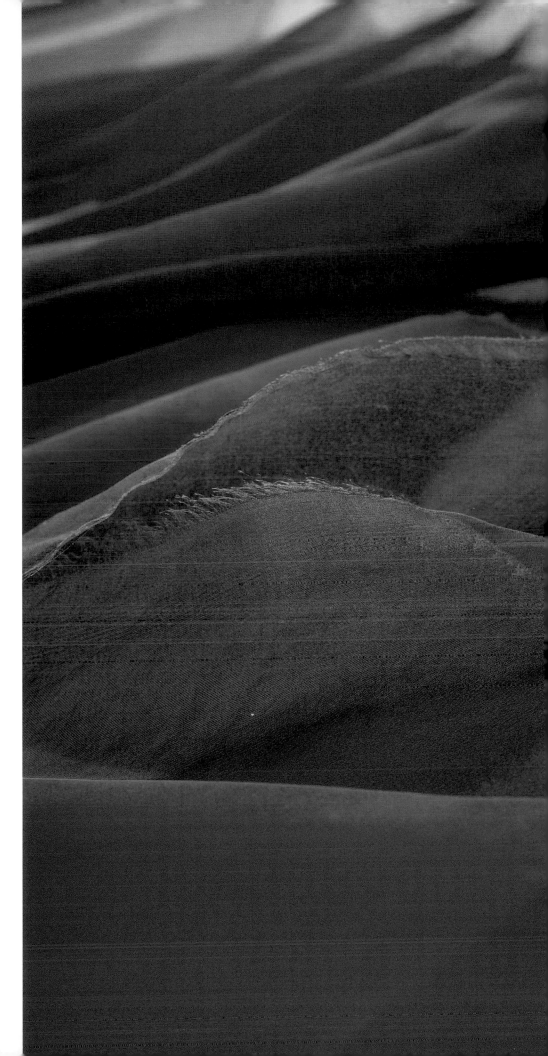

# Opacity

Having considered the opportunities associated with using transparent colour, we can now look at how opacity can be used effectively. Most papers, fabrics and threads have opaque qualities. In other words, light does not shine through them. When a piece of yellow paper is placed on top of a blue sheet, for example, it remains yellow, unlike a sheet of yellow cellophane or acetate which appears green. As mentioned previously, most paint and fabric colours are transparent, and it is important to evaluate the strength of the base colour and consider how the top colour will appear when printed. By adding some form of opacity to the top colour, it will remain a truer colour.

When dealing with paint on paper, a small amount of white paint or gesso applied to the top layer will mask the ground colour. When printing on a dark fabric, use an opaque fabric colour or add some white to the print colour. These methods will mask the ground colour, allowing you to layer colours on to a dark background.

When layering coloured fabrics, it is fun to explore the possibilities of layering transparent fabrics such as organza or chiffon with pieces of opaque fabric such as felt or close-woven cotton.

**Right:** *Dyed cotton organdie, monoprinted with opaque scarlet, magenta and yellow fabric paint, then cut and machine stitched.*

# Translucency

Translucent colour often confuses people as it falls between transparent and opaque colour. It allows light through it but it is not totally clear. It has a slightly misty quality, like tracing paper; you can see a shape through it, but it is not clearly defined. Certain media will give translucent effects, such as matt medium, as will certain papers, such as abaca tissue and lightweight lokta paper. A number of fabrics can be considered to be translucent, such as voiles, organdie, silk, cotton batiste and silk georgette.

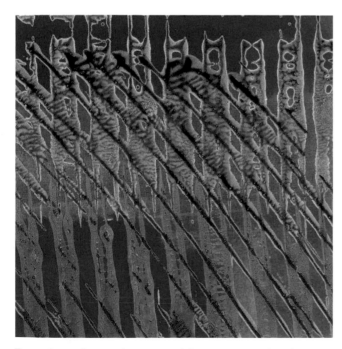

*Turquoise, yellow and green varnish were monoprinted on to white cartridge paper, then magenta and golden yellow ink were applied.*

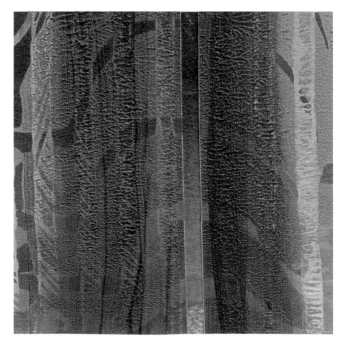

*A lemon yellow acrylic monoprint had turquoise ink applied then, once dry, a yellow and a magenta varnish were added to create greens and violets as well as oranges and reds.*

# Exploring layers

I love collating colour ideas in my sketchbooks. I gradually build layers of rich, transparent colour over opaque print and, as the colour starts to glow, it fills me with happiness. These layered effects can be achieved in numerous ways. Always think about the contrasts between two colours: is one naturally lighter or darker than the other? Can this be altered by adding white or opacity or by making one of the colours transparent? When printing, perhaps the top colour can be scratched into before it is dry, thus revealing the base colour.

**Below:** *Painting of sweet peas and nasturtiums using inks, small areas of Markal Paintstik plus a little diluted white acrylic on watercolour paper.*

Using the qualities of transparency, opacity and translucency in your work sounds complex, but the added depth and richness of colour they allow you to achieve in colourful compositions makes them well worth exploring. Take care not to let the piece become too dark too quickly as it is difficult to bring light areas back into a piece once the paper is saturated with inks. The more practice and experimentation you do with these media and techniques, the more confident you become with your use of colour.

**Below:** *Vibrant floral colours reflect the bright sunlight and deep shadows experienced when painting with inks and resists in a garden in France. The inks dried quickly in the hot sunshine, enabling me to layer the inks, getting the colour darker and even more intense.*

# Recording colour

As you learn more about colour, you will start to see colour combinations everywhere. In order to be able to use these in your work it is important to make careful records of them in your sketchbook so that you can reproduce them true to your original observation at a later date.

SWEET
WILLIAMS

POPPIES
JULY

Acrylic.

Phthalo Blue
Ultramarine
Pyrrol red light
Quinacridone
Magenta

Quinacridone,
Crimson

Hansa Yellow Medium

**Below:** *Observations of poppies and Sweet Williams, using inks as transparent colour with layers of opaque acrylic colour to give contrast.*

acrylic

Flowers can be a good reference for understanding specific colours. A summer flowerbed full of Sweet Williams and unusual poppies, for example, provides an ideal opportunity to study different reds and greens. In the early autumn, especially after a damp summer, gardens suddenly have areas of amazing, uncontrollable colour. In my garden, long, glorious stems of violet, lilac and mauve sweet-pea flowers appear, and at the same time climbing nasturtiums in a blaze of oranges, chrome yellows and reds are rampaging across paths and up walls and steps. The colour combinations of these flowers are magical, but very difficult to describe in words. It is far easier to photograph them as a way of recording the colours, but when you take a photograph are you really looking or even seeing what colours are there? It is much harder to observe the flowers closely, to analyse the colours and try to reproduce them in paint, but this method is by far the most satisfying and exciting.

## USING LIQUID COLOUR

Liquid colour is a good medium for recording colour. It is easy to alter a colour slightly, making it bluer, redder or even yellower, but it is also very easy to make the colours too dark, heavy or even muddy. As explained on pages 40–41, certain colours will dominate others, thus deadening their luminosity, freshness or even their delicacy.

When painting outdoors in warm weather, I use dye powders dissolved in water and painted directly on to watercolour paper. The inks dry quickly, so that working from light to dark, the colours can be built up in layers. As the inks are transparent, every colour addition will darken the previous colour, and the overall effect will be to make the colours darker and richer. This will give definition, but sometimes the vibrancy of the original colours is lost. By layering some very bright colours like yellows and reds, strong oranges can be achieved.

Darker areas are worked using a fine brush to give added detail and contrast. Occasionally I use a Markal Paintstik to give areas of resist and slight texture. To finish, I mix acrylic colours and apply further layers, either in blocks or painted on in short brushstrokes. My aim is to capture quickly the energy and vibrancy of the colours, not necessarily shapes or forms.

I use a good-quality watercolour paper so that different colours can be applied in specific areas as well as being allowed to bleed into each other when I want them to. Sometimes I wet the paper first so that the colour can be introduced gradually and allowed to run and fade into the paper, giving subtle tints.

I use a limited colour palette and make myself mix the colours that I need. Working with scarlet, golden yellow, violet, a small amount of magenta and medium blue ink, for example, I can mix a wide range of colours. The golden yellow and scarlet can be used to create numerous reds, vermilions, gingers, oranges and deep yellows as well as light peaches and creams when additional water is added or a little bit of white acrylic.

Foliage greens can be made by mixing golden yellow with small additions of medium blue. They range from green yellow ochre through to wonderful, slightly misty green-greys. The colours for the sweet-pea flowers, shown on page 64, are mixed using different proportions of violet, medium blue and a touch of magenta. Varying quantities of water are added to dilute the intensity of the colour.

# Using paper collage

Previously I have suggested that making coloured squares using paper collage helps you to identify variations in colour (see page 43). I find that collage is a very good way of recording ideas; to 'draw' and create textural surfaces.

## Selecting papers

I begin by gathering together a variety of different papers that I know will cut and tear well. First I select papers that will absorb ink easily such as lightweight cartridge paper, lightweight lokta paper, medium-weight kozo as well as abaca tissue and very lightweight lens tissue. Both lokta and kozo paper are Asian handmade papers. They absorb ink beautifully, giving rich, glowing colours when dry. Kozo is a soft, almost felt-like paper that needs to be pulled apart rather than torn, whereas lokta is a crisp, fibrous paper that will tear well, if sometimes unevenly.

Cartridge paper, abaca and lens tissue are all machine-manufactured papers that have an evenly finished surface, giving a consistent tear. Abaca will become translucent when dry and lens tissue is even more delicate and slightly more transparent. They are excellent for layering, creating strong, rich colours, but their delicacy means that when applying liquid colour, it is advisable to lay them on another sheet of paper, such as cartridge paper, to give them stability. Apply the ink gently with a soft brush or sponge brush and only lift off the backing paper when they are completely dry.

*Right: Sketchbook page, on which layers of ink and varnish have been applied. I was looking at the various effects I could achieve by layering papers and applying inks, blots from wet papers and varnish. Further papers, lens tissue and abaca tissue were manipulated and glued on to give a floral impression.*

*Left: Dye-painted abaca paper, lens tissue and lokta paper.*

I will also collect together papers that colour well with acrylic and Markal Paintstiks. Cartridge paper, lightweight khadi cotton-rag paper and medium-weight lokta paper are excellent surfaces for these media. I apply the acrylic with a print roller or by brushing the colour into the paper surface, depending on how much texture I require. I mix two colours together, perhaps starting with scarlet and gradually adding ultramarine to give various russets, gingers, mauves and deep purple blues. As I print or paint, I will add differing quantities of white to give a whole range of coloured tints such as peaches, terracotta, mauve-greys and light indigo. This way I can achieve subtle, moody colours as well as stronger, more vibrant colours.

I colour areas of cartridge and lokta paper with Markal Paintstiks, using professional colours such as phthalo blue and adding titanium white, working the colour into the surface of the paper to give a shiny, oily finish. By using my fingers to rub the colour into the paper surface, I can vary the density and shade of the colour.

Afterwards, the acrylic and Markal Paintstik can be over-inked to give variety of colour and tone to the paper surface. It is fun applying these colours, preparing papers by adjusting the colours as well as the surfaces. Once dry, cut or tear the papers up into small pieces. By sorting them roughly into colours and storing them in transparent bags, they will be ready for use when you have the opportunity to do some collage work.

Quickly gluing a small strip of coloured paper, rolling another strip into position and then rapidly tearing another scrap is fun. Always start in the background, building the image towards the front, layering up the colour. If possible, prepare your own coloured papers. This process is both illuminating and challenging. Try painting or printing acrylic on to newspaper or applying ink to different tissues such as lens and abaca tissue. Printing acrylic on to lightweight lokta paper then painting it with inks results in a coloured paper that tears and rolls nicely in your fingers when dry.

*Right: A sketchbook page on which ink has been blotted from an unusual paper that I was experimenting with. A collage, using a wide variety of inked, printed and Markal-coloured torn papers, has then been superimposed on top. A wide variety of papers has been used, including commercially coloured flat paper, lightweight inked lokta paper, and coloured lokta with acrylic printing, acrylic wax and a little lustre powder.*

# Tip

As you handle coloured papers, tearing, cutting and manipulating them, you will become familiar with their qualities. Some give crisp tears; others fray; some tear unevenly because of their random, fibrous composition; and some roll and twist beautifully in your fingers to give fine, sinuous lines.

*Left: A collage created as a happy by-product of preparing acrylic-coloured papers. The newspaper protecting the table had a wonderful vibrancy where the colours had spilled off the paper. How often do the 'background' papers look so exciting!*

# Making a paper collage

Begin by selecting a medium-weight, smooth, white cartridge paper that will not buckle too easily when it has numerous layers of paper glued to it. Sort out the colours that you think you are going to need for your piece of work. Use a glue that you are comfortable with. I use either PVA glue or Coccoina, a ready-prepared glue paste. PVA is a fairly thick, white glue that needs to be spread with a palette knife or old brush. It dries clear with a slight sheen. It is very sticky, so I find it best to lay the coloured papers on an old newspaper when applying the glue. Coccoina comes in a small tin with a little brush and is very easy to apply; it does not seem to leave a surface sheen. Some of the very lightweight papers require careful handling as they become more delicate and fragile when wet. They also become more transparent when glue is applied.

Start your collage by looking for some papers that will work as a background. Carefully study the subject you are 'drawing' and, having decided which colours are furthest away from you, select some large areas of these colours to divide up the background roughly. Do not make it too detailed at this stage; a broad area of colour will be fine as you will be adding other papers on top. I sometimes choose papers with a variety of colours or perhaps some subtle printing for this background layer to suggest texture or distant patterning.

Next, look at the composition of the 'drawing' and roughly place, in your mind, the key areas of interest. Then select the next layers of paper. In the case of a foliage and floral collage, these layers will consist of areas of leaves, distant shadows and floral shapes, without being too detailed. The pieces can be quite crudely torn or cut at this stage, as they are suggestions of shapes rather than accurate representations. More background colours that are slightly darker or lighter than the first ones can also be applied to give variety and texture. Abaca tissue can be excellent for background areas, as it can be layered to give a variety of colours and tones, as well as giving a nice, subtle texture.

In the next layer, start to introduce the more detailed areas of your subject. For example, begin to work in the flower heads, along with some foreground foliage. Select the position of each focal point to apply the details and build up specific areas such as stems, leaves and flowers.

If you have selected a background colour that is too strong and dark, it could show through any translucent papers that you have placed on top, making it difficult to achieve vibrancy in the foreground. In this case, try inserting an opaque, lighter paper, like a layer or mask, and then cover it with the translucent paper. This method can give added depth and vibrancy to the finished composition.

Gradually, as you build layers of papers on to the surface of the picture, a composition emerges. All the time you are tearing and gluing paper, you can adjust the composition and, more importantly, your own personal application of colour. How you place one piece of paper adjacent to, on top of or under another will alter the overall appearance of your composition. Colour can be enriched and given emphasis with tiny scraps of rolled, scrunched or torn paper.

Always stand back from your work regularly and view it from a short distance to see how the colours are working together and how the composition is developing. You may have to adjust your work by adding more lighter or darker papers.

**Above:** *Nasturtiums and sweet peas built up in collage using printed, inked and manipulated papers including cartridge, abaca and lens tissue.*

# Taking collage into fabric and stitch

Having achieved a satisfactory paper collage, you may wish to explore the subject further by interpreting it in fabric and stitch. Understanding the transparency, translucency and opacity of different materials, both paper and fabric, is vital if you wish to add depth and interest to a piece of work.

## Making a fabric collage

Starting with the background, select a few specific fabrics to indicate the feel and colour of the distant areas of the composition. I like to use a reasonably firm fabric as a backing, quite close woven but soft enough for easy stitching as I may wish to use some heavier threads later on. I often use a lightweight calico or white cotton organdie. Tack your base fabrics into position, giving broad 'brushstrokes' of colour. More permanent stitching can be applied later. By working your fabric collages using loose tacking stitches initially, you will have the flexibility to manipulate the materials and model the shapes into position as your work progresses.

**Left:** *Paper collage of nasturtiums and sweet peas, using mainly abaca tissue and lens tissue with occasional layers of coloured cartridge paper.*

**Right:** *Stitched fabric collage using silk organza and silk chiffon on top of layers of silk and viscose rib, viscose satin, cotton organdie, silk muslin and cotton muslin. In this piece, I wanted to explore the qualities and characteristics of different fabrics. I discovered that silk crepeline is more transparent than silk organza, that chiffon has a softness that gives both depth and delicacy, and that cotton organdie produces crisp, structural elements. I didn't need to bond the fabrics as they were easy to catch-stitch to a backing fabric, and the surface did not become stiff but remained soft and easy to hand sew.*

Having laid down a basic structure, but still working on the background areas, begin to introduce variations of colour and tone, perhaps using small areas of silk chiffon to add subtle tonal changes or to create darker areas. Sometimes these areas can be little fabric scraps that are twisted and manipulated to suggest background shapes such as leaves or shadows. Carefully move these fragments into position and attach them with tiny, almost invisible stitches. Do not be too precise at this stage – there should be suggestions of shapes rather than specific forms, as they are in the background.

As the piece develops, gradually build the composition by layering fabrics that are cut and torn into suitable shapes, manipulated into position and stitched down. Sometimes a careful fold or perhaps a cut on the cross of the fabric, will give an incredibly smooth, sensuous curve. This can be counterbalanced by a raw edge that ripples or flutters loosely on the surface of the piece. Each fabric will have its own characteristics that you can utilise to give depth and feeling to your composition. It can be great fun experimenting and handling the fabric, and making it do what you want.

Ultimately, fabric collages can be left simply as manipulated fabric with holding stitches, or they can form the basis for more elaborate stitched surfaces. I have found it fascinating to work with the different fabrics that I have dyed. Cutting, tearing and manipulating them makes you aware of their different qualities. The nature of the different fibres – crisp, soft, matt or shiny – becomes more evident when they are placed together in a single piece, and the variations in their density, transparency, translucency and opacity give tremendous surface interest to your work. It is a fascinating area, with so much to explore and so much more to understand.

# Selecting fabrics

The first stage of any stitched collage is to sort out the most suitable fabrics and colours. If you are working on a small scale, say 25cm (10in) square, select fine, flexible fabrics that can be layered and manipulated with ease, including a variety of woven fabrics of various densities and fibres. When you have sorted through your bags of coloured and dyed fabrics and made a selection, iron the fabric pieces you have chosen to familiarise yourself with them; you need to know how they will behave when stitched into your composition.

**Right and below:** *I created a series of three layered and stitched fabric pieces exploring a range of dyed greens. Each piece had additional stitch incorporating different colours – violet, pink and blue – to see the effects these colour have.*

**Opposite:** *Detail of the piece shown bottom right.*

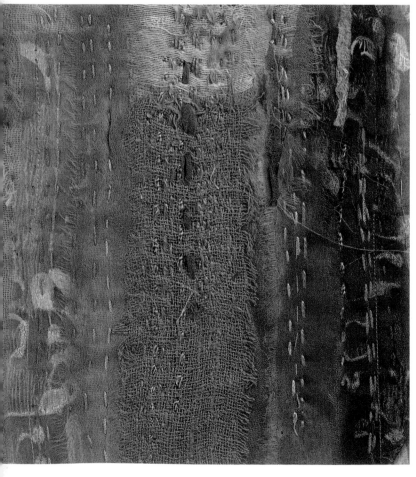

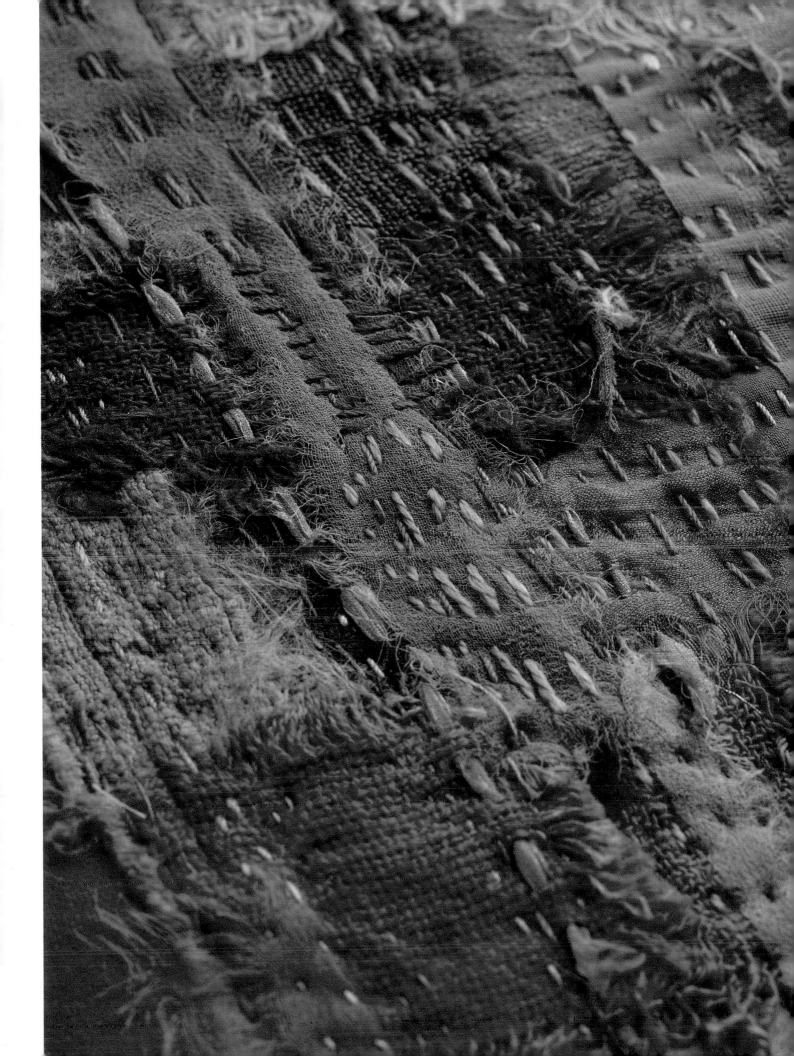

The different densities of the weave, the drape, the handle, sheen and opacity are all important. Different fabrics will behave in a variety of different ways. Stiff cotton organdie can be folded, pleated, rolled and curled into crisp, dominant shapes, whereas delicate silk chiffon will flop and curl gently, giving voluptuous curves and subtle shadows. Some fabrics are very opaque, such as close-woven cotton poplin, giving strong, even colour, whereas silk organza will be almost transparent and can give neat, controlled shapes. Silk crepeline is very transparent and is hardly visible when layered over strong colours, but when placed selectively it can give intriguing tonal shadows. All the transparent and semi-transparent fabrics can be layered successfully to give subtle gradations of colour. Fabrics that have a high gloss such as a rich viscose or silk satin will add light and dimension to the stitched surface as well as rich colour.

I love to work with fabrics that can be dip-dyed or dye-painted with cold-water dyes. Fabrics such as cotton organdie, silk organza, silk crepeline, silk chiffon, silk mousseline, silk and cotton muslin, silk and viscose mixtures, as well as cotton muslin and fine cotton lawn, all dye beautifully.

It is always worth dyeing short lengths of fine threads when dyeing fabric. Create small skeins of threads, tie them at one end to prevent tangling and then immerse or dangle them into the dye in your palette and see them wick up the colour.

I prefer to work fabric collages by hand as it allows me finer and more subtle control than would be achievable with a sewing machine. A delicate shape, for example, can be held in position with a single stitch – something that would not be possible with machine stitching.

# Working with coloured fabric strips

I will often arrange coloured fabrics by cutting and tearing them into strips, then machining or hand stitching them in lines, turning them and overlaying them as I work. Sometimes I will seam them together to conceal all the raw edges; other times I will deliberately leave the raw edges exposed, even laying two or three pieces together to enjoy the colour buzz that a frayed edge can give to the whole colour experience.

Working with coloured strips of fabric can be very liberating. Try to work intuitively rather than planning the order of the fabric strips before you stitch, and be aware of the effects of each colour on another as you work.

*Layers of pink and lime fabrics seamed together, mainly using raw edges. The fabrics are all lightweight, such as fine silk and cotton, loose-woven linen, silk and viscose rib, and cotton lawn.*

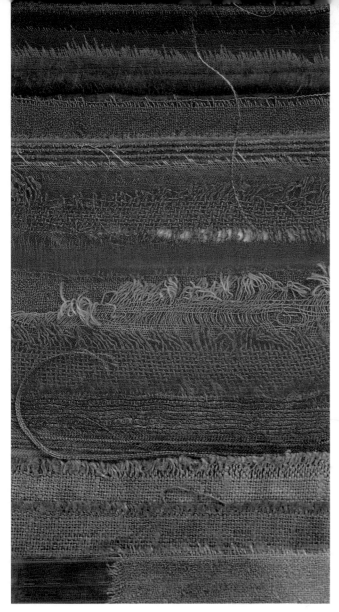

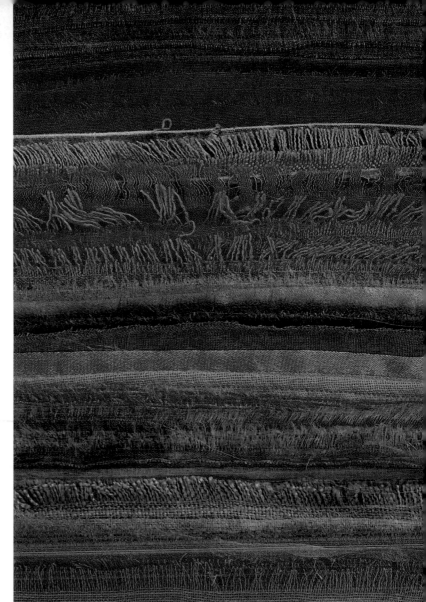

**Above:** *Keeping a record of a fabric selection in a sketchbook can be really useful. This one consists of fabric strips glued on to the page, including silk and viscose, cotton organdie, silk noil, silk and viscose rib, silk noil scrim, cotton muslin, tussah silk and linen, all dyed in Procion MX dye.*

**Above and opposite:** *The same fabrics as those detailed on the left plus a small piece of blue viscose silk satin, all seamed together using turned as well as raw edges. Some colours were used repeatedly. This sample is shown in close up opposite.*

Sometimes I arrange the scraps of coloured fabric in a sketchbook, simply gluing them in place, but my preferred method is stitch. To make a fabric piece in this way, first pin or tack the fabrics into position, considering whether each fabric needs to have the raw edges hidden or gently rolled under, or whether the edges should be frayed to give a slightly filtered colour. Different weights of fabric will give a variety of colour effects, as will their surface qualities. You may prefer to bond your fabrics in place so that you can stitch easily across the surface. This is helpful if you want to keep everything in position and can give a very finished result. Personally, I rarely use this method, preferring instead to work with the different fabrics' personalities; their ability to become slightly loose, rough or even unravel and thus give surface interest and variety to my work.

Once the fabrics are arranged and pinned or tacked in position, they can be secured with hand or machine stitching. Hand stitching is more versatile, for example stitches can be concealed or different types of stitching used, such running stitch or couching, to achieve greater colour emphasis.

When using a sewing machine, wind a number of bobbins with various colours and change the thread colour frequently. This will give you greater variety and more subtle colour combinations. Additional machine stitching can be used to add an extra colour dimension using simple couching, fine satin stitch or rows of straight stitch.

# Taking inspiration from other artists

Looking at good colour reproductions of different artists' work can be an invaluable exercise. It might seem like the kind of thing you were made to do as a student or even at school, but really looking at a particular painting can provide a rich seam of information.

   I often look through books on wonderful artists and collect postcards of their work. Sometimes I look at how the colour is applied, layered and mixed. It is fascinating as you begin to see how many layers of colour have been placed over each other, and how the proportion of colour is so vital to give a rich hue. As you look, the more you see or even choose to ignore.

   Sometimes I will take an area of a favourite postcard and translate it into a simple collage. By limiting the size and working quickly, adjusting the colours without labouring over them, the piece becomes more spontaneous, retaining a freshness that larger, more closely worked pieces can lack.

*A small paper collage of various painted papers, using* Arabs 1 (1909) *by Wassily Kandinsky as inspiration.*

Once you have made a paper collage, take your collaged colour scheme into fabric and stitch. Follow the method I described in the previous section, on pages 74–75.

Using the same fabric selection as shown on page 80, I took a square of cotton organdie as a backing and began to attach the fabrics to it with simple slip stitches. Starting with the background, I applied some basic areas of colour – orange shading to blue, and a sandy yellow cotton organdie with a dark layer of silk organza in front. The edges of these fabrics were turned to give a firm edge and hence a strong line. These were contrasted with pieces of fabric on the left that have frayed edges to give softness and a slightly blurred look. Blue cotton organdie was twisted into strips and caught down to represent a tree. Further areas of fabric were applied – some single thickness, some double thickness, some with raw edges, some turned – each giving a different surface and colour intensity. Finally, limited areas of fine stitching were added.

*A loosely referenced fabric interpretation of the paper collage shown on the left.*

# Exploring other colour collections

T hroughout my teaching career, I have shared different dyeing processes with numerous students. Often I will take the opportunity to dye my own fabrics at the same time as my students are dyeing theirs, and these are sometimes over-dyed as well. The over-dyeing produces a variety of different shades of one colour, and the result is a beautiful coloured collection. For instance, violet will achieve deep maroon, aubergine, mauve, wine and deep russets from over-dyeing scarlet, ultramarine, turquoise and magenta. Over-dyeing these colours with jet black will produce a range of slate greys, steel, misty and stormy colours. By trimming these pieces into uniform squares and applying them to a similar ginger and violet background, another colourful piece is produced.

**Above:** *Detail of the cushion on the right, showing linen and viscose satin in greys, violets and rusty oranges surrounded by orange cotton organdie that has been applied by machine.*

**Above:** *Cushion made of dyed and over-dyed linen, viscose and cotton fabrics. The squares were attached to a backing using satin stitch and then edged with either dark orange or violet cotton organdie to provide emphasis and an unpredictable finish.*

# Exploring violets and oranges with blue-greens

Colour combinations are endless, but it is still exciting to explore the possibilities. When working with liquid colour, the results are quick and it is easy to lose the power and energy of one colour by being too generous with another. You need to retain an element of control, being careful how you select colours and considering the order in which you apply them. When working with fabric, thread and stitch, the whole process is much slower.

In this piece, I selected specific background colours to create strong colour contrast, in this case violet cotton with some squares of orange, dark salmon and deep pink linen. Hand stitching was then added, which has infused the piece with energy and variety by turning the stitches in different directions and using a variety of weights and finishes of thread. The colours were adjusted as I worked across the piece.

**Below and opposite:**
*Linen squares hand stitched with a variety of different threads in a range of blues and greens. It was exciting to evaluate not only the different colours of the threads but also their various qualities.*

# Exploring reds, oranges and greens

One of the colour combinations that I find quite difficult is green and red. Both these colours can be very strong and dominant. They can also be quite dark and rich in pigment colour. I decided to explore this colour combination using monoprinting on scoured cotton and cotton organdie. I used fabric paints and mixed the colours from a lemon yellow, turquoise and magenta. I also used white as I needed to add tints and opacity.

**This page and opposite:** *Each of these four fabric samples initially had golden yellow and magenta fabric paints applied separately to it. The colours were then layered in different ways using monoprinting, roller printing, brushing and masking and the occasional addition of a small amount of white. Finally, limited areas of a contrasting light green were added.*

# MONOPRINTING

Monoprinting can give a wonderful variety of different marks as well as subtle variations in colour. Sometimes I will roll the colour directly on to the fabric; other times I will brush the colour on to the monoprinting sheet and then gently print it on to the fabric surface. You need to clean your monoprinting plate regularly so that you can see the colour changes, especially when you want to vary the colour across a printed area.

To create the look shown in the examples here and on pages 90 and 91, start with an undyed background fabric and apply colour with a print roller. Then cut square masks and use masking tape to give straight lines and simple units. Apply a few blocks of lemon yellow and gradually added magenta to it, which gives a range of different oranges and reds. Some of the colour emphasis is created by gently brushing colour from a right angle of masking tape.

**Above and opposite:** *A square of printed scoured cotton was layered with wadding, then stitched first by machine and then by hand. Straight machine stitch was initially applied using light green thread, then fine green knitting yarn was couched down with zig-zag stitching and a blind hem stitch (see the detail opposite). After this, a limited area of hand running stitch with fine silk was used to give additional emphasis in the upper part of the piece. Finally, the square was bound with a shaded piece of green scoured cotton to finish the piece.*

As you print, gradually adjust the colours, working in this series with mixes of yellow, magenta and an occasional touch of white.

Once you are happy with the background, add limited areas of green mixed from lemon yellow, white and small quantities of turquoise. Try brushing the greens every now and then from a cut or torn mask to give a strong edge on one side. Deliberately masking an area and then carefully applying drawn lines from the monoprinting sheet can also be very effective.

Once the printing is complete, these pieces of fabric are ready for additional coloured stitching, either by machine or hand. An example of a finished stitched piece is shown above.

# Exploring oranges, mauve and magenta

Beautiful pieces of dyed and printed fabrics should never be hidden away in a cupboard unused. This luscious piece of dye-painted viscose satin simply glows with colour. By bonding squares of mauve monoprinted cotton organdie to the surface, the glowing colours seem even richer. By machine couching some space-dyed threads in simple stripes across the surface, a delicious colour combination appears. The sheen of the fabric coupled with simple squares of colour and a limited amount of surface stitching makes an excellent centrepiece for future work.

**Below and opposite:** *Dye-painted viscose satin cushion with a central panel of monoprinted cotton organdie, with machine-couched space-dyed threads to add contrasting colour and surface texture.*

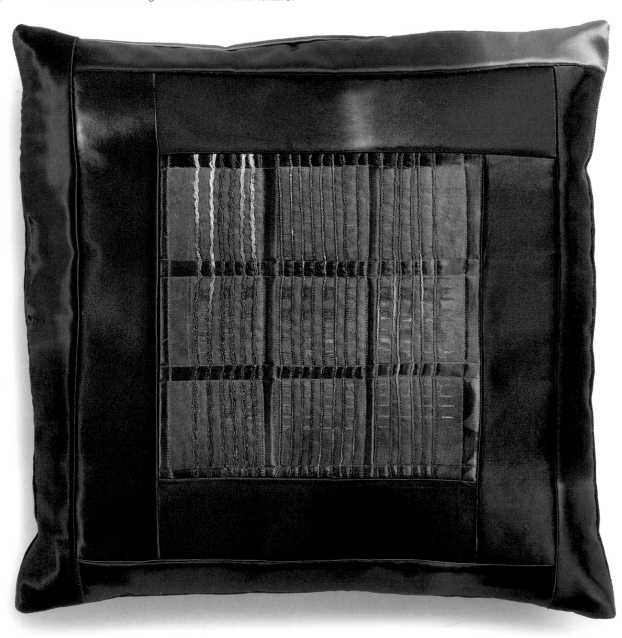

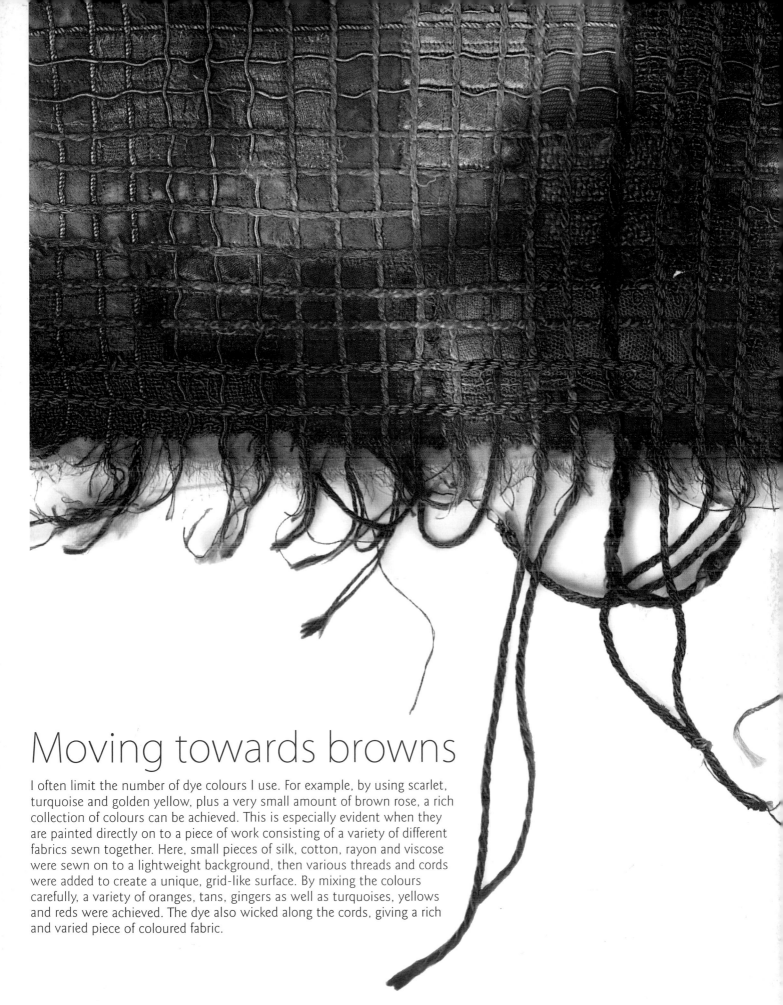

# Moving towards browns

I often limit the number of dye colours I use. For example, by using scarlet, turquoise and golden yellow, plus a very small amount of brown rose, a rich collection of colours can be achieved. This is especially evident when they are painted directly on to a piece of work consisting of a variety of different fabrics sewn together. Here, small pieces of silk, cotton, rayon and viscose were sewn on to a lightweight background, then various threads and cords were added to create a unique, grid-like surface. By mixing the colours carefully, a variety of oranges, tans, gingers as well as turquoises, yellows and reds were achieved. The dye also wicked along the cords, giving a rich and varied piece of coloured fabric.

# A brown-rose collection

Dyeing a fabric collection can be both fascinating and rewarding. I will often decide to dye a collection focusing on variations in a specific colour. Though I love to work with primary and secondary colours, there are times when I want to introduce slightly deeper and subtle versions, particularly in the darker, moodier sector of the colour wheel. I find that the addition of a brown-rose dye colour can give gloriously deep, rich colours. The warmth of this brown works beautifully with the blue sector of the colour wheel.

**Above:** *A collection of fabrics dyed using brown rose mixed with ultramarine, violet and turquoise.*

**Left:** *Stitched piece using a blue screen print and fine stitchery. Once the stitching had been added, the original fabric seemed to be an even richer colour. The deep ultramarine seemed more violet and the brown appeared redder, more luscious and fruity. The colour of the stitching has depth and movement, especially when contrasted with the light blue.*

**Right:** *Detail of stitching, showing the variations in thread weight.*

Deciding to dye a specific selection of fabrics can form part of the planning for a project. For this particular collection I decided to use three fabrics: scoured cotton, cotton organdie and silk noil. Scoured cotton is an evenly woven, medium-weight fabric and is slightly cream in colour. Cotton organdie has a crisp, fine weave, dyes very well and is excellent for stitching and manipulating. It is translucent, so it can be used to create some wonderful layered effects. Silk noil has a slightly rough surface. It absorbs dye well, giving rich, dark colours. When the three fabrics are dyed and then laid together, the scoured cotton will appear slightly lighter, the silk noil has a rich surface colour and the cotton organdie has a flat, strong colour.

I dyed the fabrics in plastic bags using brown-rose dye with either ultramarine, violet or turquoise. I varied the proportions of the colours, sometimes using fifty per cent of each colour and other times using a thirty per cent to seventy per cent mixture. Once the fabrics had been rinsed, I had achieved rich brown, violet, mauve, burgundy, light purple and deep violet colours. When laid together, folded and arranged in rows, they make a beautiful collection, ready to use.

I selected some of the dyed cotton organdie pieces to screen print with a pale blue grid pattern. I then bonded one print on to another dye-painted piece that had been painted with mixes of brown rose and ultramarine in simple stripes. These fabrics were laid on to two further cotton organdie layers, both dyed browns, which helped to make the colour richer. Finally, these surfaces were hand stitched with a series of circular images using a variety of reds and oranges and a small area of light blue.

# Practical applications: foliage series

I often start a piece of work by spending some time printing on paper. I then use inks and resists to give extra depth of colour, or draw into the print with coloured pencils and pastels. Exploring design ideas using different 'drawing' techniques on papers such as printing, inking and resists all help to inform your choice of technique when you come to work with fabric.

Some techniques are transferred easily from paper to fabric – once you have created a print block, for example, it can be used on paper as well as on fabric. Try using the same techniques, but in different areas or in a different order. The behaviour of liquid colour depends on the qualities of the surface to which it is applied, so the choice of fabric or fibre, its surface and finish, are crucial to the final result. Try to choose a fine, reasonably closely woven material for good absorption of the dye and well-defined prints. Too much repeated printing can stiffen the fabric, which might make it difficult to stitch. Take care, therefore, not to apply thick, heavy layers of print.

The pieces in my foliage series build gradually from a core of selected pattern and colour. The manipulation of the fabric surface and its combination with stitch and areas of print allow me to create rich and unusual colour combinations.

**Opposite:** *Block and roller print from a foliage design. Layers of print were enhanced with coloured varnish, Markal Paintstiks and repeated layers of ink.*

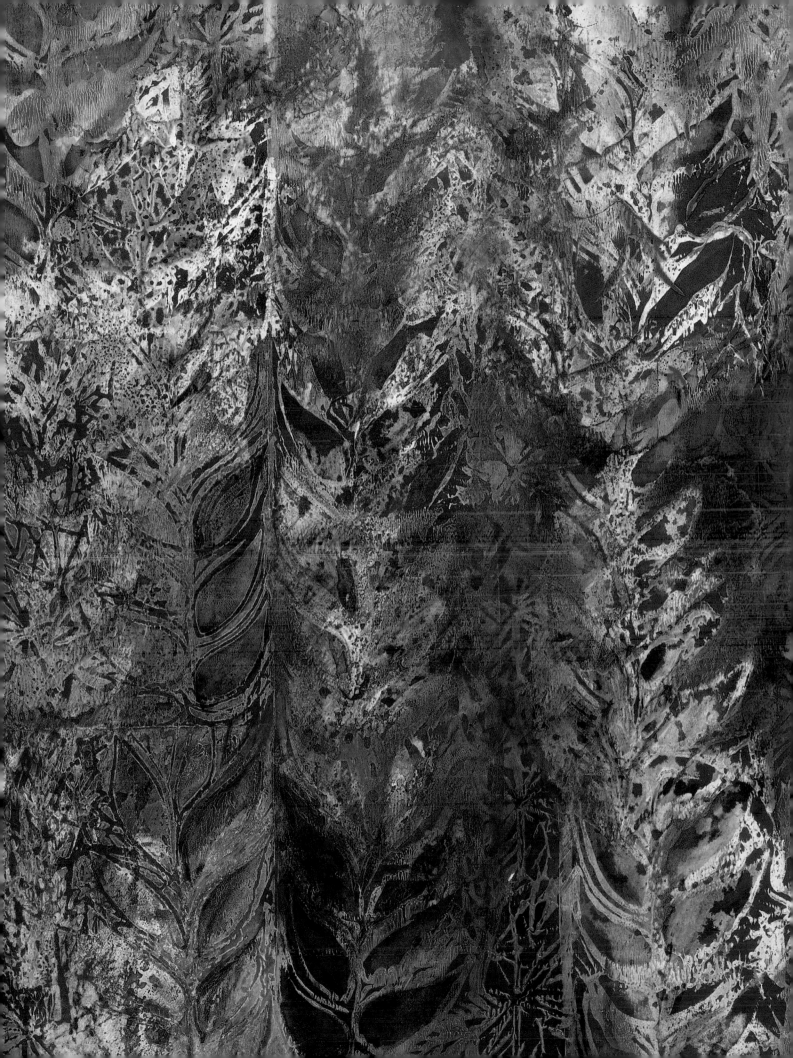

# Working with violets and oranges

## PRINTING ON PAPER

I developed this series using a foliage print block that I designed and cut myself. My starting point with any printed composition is to decide on the positions of the areas of printing, which depend on where I wish to have pattern and where I want areas of rich, plain colour. I usually start printing with a fairly light colour on white paper. This lays the foundation for the rest of the piece.

## LAYING AN INK WASH

Once the printing is positioned, in this case using a very pale blue and a delicate lilac, and once it is completely dry, I might use a clear varnish or Markal Paintstiks that will resist the ink washes I intend to lay on top. I then work an ink across the paper and the printed areas. Here I used scarlet and golden yellow. As the ink is absorbed into the paper the colour changes, lightening slightly, and the ink adheres to some areas of the printing. It is interesting to observe the colour in relation to the printed areas. Sometimes the ink dries on to the print, but it can be wiped away easily with a damp cloth. By applying inks gradually, mixing the scarlet and yellow, perhaps adding a small amount of blue to darken the reds slightly, the whole piece begins to come together.

## ADDING DEFINITION WITH PASTEL

I leave the piece to dry thoroughly and then much later I return to look at the piece. The background is now a rich, bright scarlet; orange and deep, warm, blue-chestnut. The printing is very pale blue, light lilacs and some white. I then select a deep lavender pastel pencil and I draw on to the print to add definition and emphasis to the printed shapes. I draw firm lines, but also rub the colour into the print surface, giving a range of different lilacs, lavenders, pale violets and even subtle greys. Occasionally, in a small area I use a sharp contrast such as a vibrant green blended with a deep indigo blue or a deep purple with a bit of scarlet.

Working on paper is a pleasurable and fascinating experience. Each colour that is added can alter the overall colour effect, and it is very easy to over-ink the piece or put on additional layers of resist or drawn colour. It is therefore important to keep standing back and evaluating the effects you have achieved. All this helps to make you aware of different colour combinations as well as the placement of specific colour details, which is invaluable when preparing work for stitching.

## ADDING STITCHING

Machine stitching can be added selectively to paper prints, especially if they are on strong paper such as cotton-rag paper. I tend to use very simple machine stitches, mainly linear, working often with the foot off or a darning foot on and the feed dogs down. This allows you to move the paper in any direction easily. The machine-stitched lines give another dimension to the paper surface that it is not possible to achieve by drawing. These lines can be either stitched repeatedly to build the colour or used selectively to give extra emphasis here and there.

**Right:** *Machine stitching can add an extra dimension to paper prints. Here I have used bright yellow in some areas to lighten them, and in other places I have used a deep maroon to emphasise the shaded areas. Finally, I used lilac stitching to give limited areas of decorative patterning to some of the leaf shapes.*

## LAYERING THE FABRICS

The transition from paper to fabric begins by making your colour selections and layering the fabrics together. Selecting a limited colour palette of contrasting colours is a fascinating and challenging exercise. It makes you organise your fabrics, your threads and your brain. I find myself repositioning colours from reds to violets, yellows to oranges, challenging my understanding of colours as well as how to describe or categorise them.

This piece is worked in a selection of different oranges and an assortment of violets. The oranges range from bright tangerines, even a very yellowy orange, to gingers, nutmegs and turmeric colours. The darkest colour is a deep ginger, which is lively and not too dark. The violets range from deep aubergine, a reddish purple and a light mauve to a pale lavender.

Layering fabrics subtly alters the intensity or brightness of the colours. Layered colour can be cut away, lifted or turned back, revealing an additional rich seam of colour underneath. By carefully choosing the order in which you layer the colours, all kinds of different arrangements and effects can be achieved.

The design shown opposite has fairly simple shapes that are manipulated easily. The contrast of light violet, which appears warm and rich when set against the bright ginger or a burnt orange, is luscious. Using hand-dyed fabrics can give a greater variety of colour. In one piece of fabric the colours can subtly change from deep rust to pale salmon and then to a light mauve. Some of the fabrics have a subtle print, others are plain.

## CUTTING BACK THE LAYERS AND ADDING STITCH

Once the fabrics are arranged, the layers are cut back, turned under, or even laid over areas of the design, giving an opportunity to add extra colour with stitch. A sewing machine is a quick method of securing the layers of fabric together. It is easy, however, to obliterate areas of subtlety by applying too much of one colour. Using hand stitching in a simple limited palette can add vibrant contrasts or muted variations. Even the choice of stitch will alter colours. Simple running stitch can be evenly or unevenly spaced, giving two totally different appearances. Selecting a bolder chain stitch, however, will give a solid, defined line; a strong, even area of colour rather than a broken, more subtle line.

*Right:* Foliage 1, *a loose interpretation of the foliage paper prints I had made previously. I was thinking about the effect of counterchange, in which colours in different sections of a design are swapped, but I didn't want to apply any specific rules too rigidly. Instead, I just enjoyed the contrasting colours and the additional print and stitch.*

*Below:* *Fabrics were seamed together with additional applied threads then dye-painted using scarlet, violet and golden yellow dye.*

*Detail of* Foliage 1 *from the previous page, showing the directness of working with one fabric, cotton organdie, and machine and hand stitch.*

# Broadening the colour selection: exploring violets, yellows and greens

Having completed the first interpretation of my foliage series, I wanted to expand my colour palette and introduce a greater variety of fabric surfaces. I selected a palette of pale violets and grey-blues to contrast with strong orange-yellow, yellow ochre and a lime green. Some of these colours were achieved by layering different opaque and transparent fabrics together to give subtle colour alterations.

Initially I created a central panel of grey-blues and pale grey-violets with the printed cotton organdie laid on top. On either side of this central panel, areas of naturalistic grassy greens, strong orangey yellows and acid greens were positioned. Some pieces of printed organdie were put on to these fabrics to create a foliage pattern.

The layers of dyed fabrics give a variety of surfaces – matt, shiny, opaque and translucent. Some areas were arranged with subtle colour changes: a variety of pale violets and lilacs, highlighted by small contrasting stitches. Gradually these areas met and combined with contrasting colours such as acid and leaf greens, and deep marigold yellows. The printed surface is cut and turned, sometimes being highly visible and at other times becoming more subtle.

**Right:** Foliage 2, *a second interpretation of the foliage theme, using a broader colour range than before and a greater variety of fabric surfaces, as well as print and stitch (both machine and hand).*

**Below:** *A collection of various dyed, stitched and printed fabrics seamed together to create a luscious border.*

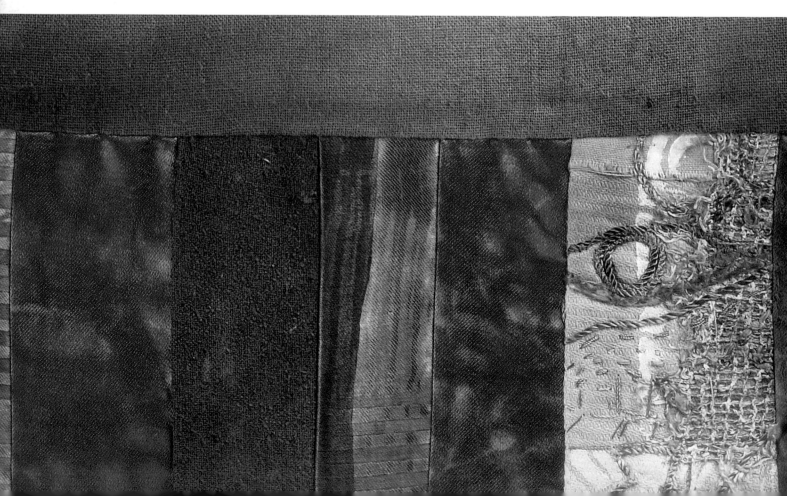

*Detail of* Foliage 2 *shown on the previous page, showing use of numerous layers of fabric, cut and turned back, and secured with both hand and machine stitch. The stitching adds little touches of detail: a red dot here, a yellow line there.*

# Taking it further: exploring multiple colour compositions

The development of my foliage series led me from a quite formal block print to a piece consisting of layers of different fabrics, hand and machine stitched, and no print at all. Numerous paper prints gave me a rich source of ideas, from which it was easy to create another interpretation of the foliage theme. The two previous pieces had an element of counterchange: placing one colour on top of another and then reversing it. I like to explore the interaction of positive and negative shapes. It is exciting to be daring; to place a limited range of colours in different relationships.

For this piece I selected dark lilacs, bright scarlets and deep yellows. I layered them together, sometimes making the lilacs dominate an area with the yellows and oranges being secondary. In an adjacent area, however, the yellows become superior with the reds and lilacs being secondary. By working in broad bands of colour, the combinations can be adjusted, with one colour taking pride of place in one area and another colour being dominant elsewhere.

## ADDING ENERGY AND EXCITEMENT

Small adjustments can add energy and excitement to your work. These are best made through experimentation rather than careful planning. It can be fun to work in this way: try adjusting the layers, bringing a particular colour to the fore, and confusing the eye sometimes by using two equally strong colours together. You may find that by bringing a sharp, contrasting line of stitch into the composition, as I have done here using turquoise, the colours start to jump about, giving excitement and energy to the whole piece. You cannot plan these effects, but somehow you know intuitively when a piece needs enlivening.

The more experimental prints and colour trials that you do, the more your confidence will grow. Keep taking a step back and viewing your work from a distance and, most importantly, sometimes be daring in your colour and fabric choices. From the initial printing on paper, to dyeing fabric and maybe printing on to it, you are arranging colours, surfaces and imagery in a way that is personal to you. Pieces grow, they alter and they gain energy, and working with them becomes addictive.

**Right:** Foliage 3 – *this piece became more complicated as it was worked. I used multiple layers of different fabrics, giving shiny, matt, transparent and soft surface finishes within the piece.*

**Below:** *An experimental paper sample using strips of monoprinted papers in scarlet, yellows and oranges that had been inked with ultramarine ink. By using strips, proportions can be altered and adjusted by eye until you are happy with the arrangement.*

This detail reveals the full range of fabrics that are included in Foliage 3 shown on the previous page. Cotton organdie is the main fabric and it helps the composition to remain stable. In addition to this there are pieces of silk mesh and layers of silk organza for depth of colour, as well as silk noil to give soft, textural areas.

# Developing design ideas

So what happens when you feel the need to start a new body of work; to leave a series behind and to move on to a new thought, theme or technique? This may be because there is a deadline for an exhibition, or the result of a series of sketchbook and paper experiments.

Developing new design ideas is always exciting; it feels like opening another door and embarking on a new adventure. My journey into townscapes involved simplifying my ideas and making dramatic, colourful statements. I worked with different proportions of colour: large areas of uninterrupted colour broken up by sudden bursts of energy in the form of contrasting colour and stitch.

## Tip
Remember: there are no rules, just a gradual nurturing of a piece of work to a colourful conclusion.

## Tip
Always save selected scraps of fabric and off-cuts of stitched pieces. They are little offerings, scraps that are still exciting. Somehow there is spontaneity; they are lively reminders of something larger, more dominant and loud. These little scraps have energy and vibrancy and need to be added to another composition.

# Townscapes

My townscapes series began as a gathering together of a small collection of fabrics, printed and inked papers, threads, and parts of a few favourite postcards selected for their use of colour. Some of the fabric pieces had been trimmed from previously finished stitched pieces, some since sold; too precious to be discarded, I knew these scraps were destined to be included in a new series. Other fabric pieces were samples made for teaching purposes or for trying out different colour combinations.

I often put together my collections on a foam core board, pinning samples in little groups of ideas. I prop these boards up where I work or where I can see them every day. It is easy to take pieces off, add others or rearrange them to explore different ideas. Below is a quick design collage incorporating squares of printed and inked papers from my collection, cut and glued together. Collages such as these can help to focus your ideas and help in the decision-making process when choosing which colours to use, and which textures and techniques to incorporate when taking your ideas into fabric and stitch.

**Below:** *A quick design collage incorporating squares of printed and inked papers from my collection, cut, torn and glued together. Notice the use of layering, with little windows cut into some of the samples and the layers underneath showing through.*

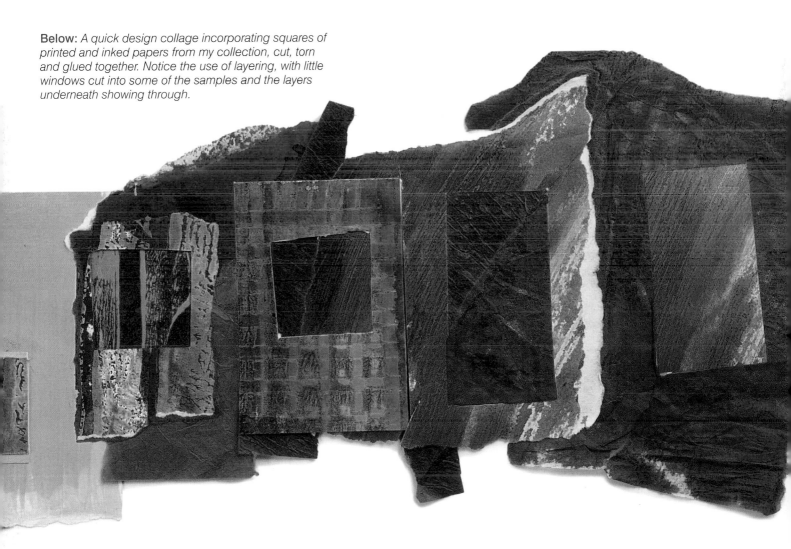

# TRANSFERRING MY COLOUR IDEAS TO FABRIC: USING PRECIOUS FRAGMENTS

Fired by this energy, I went on to explore the effect of varying the proportions of different colours using my collection of selected fabric scraps and off-cuts. The first group was made up of lightweight fabrics, hand-painted with dye. It included cotton organdie, silk organza and a silk and viscose rib. I had originally chosen to paint them with dye, so there was a variety of colour across the fabric. Areas of colour changed from dark maroon to a deep violet-blue; other pieces had a bright golden yellow and a rich, sticky apricot colour. The silk and viscose rib produced a particularly unusual effect as the dye wicked along the viscose thread producing random coloured stripes.

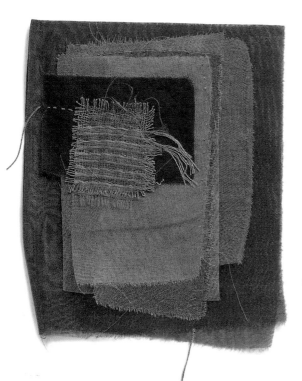

**Above:** *Layers of aquamarine and lime green, overlaid with deep red-plum cotton organdie, with a further layer of yellow cotton organdie and aquamarine silk and viscose rib stitched into position on top.*

**Right:** *Green and blue cotton organdie was used to counterbalance an intense area of layered red silk, cotton and viscose strips. This small sample was later incorporated into a much larger piece of work.*

**Above:** *An initial arrangement of blue organdies with acid yellow, leaf green, purple and pink fabric strips inserted. This was later incorporated into a larger piece of work and the fabrics used as the background for further stitch.*

**Far right:** *A small sample consisting of layers of dye-painted cotton organdie overlaid with silk organza and a square of green silk and viscose rib.*

**Right:** *Layers of dyed magenta, scarlet and yellow cotton organdie with a dense square of turquoise organdie on top. A scrap of silk and viscose rib dyed with scarlet and yellow was then stitched into position on top of the turquoise square.*

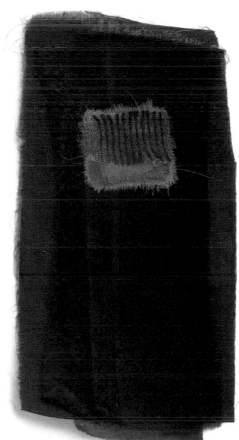

The fabrics lent themselves to a simple composition of rectangular and square areas layered into position. Some of the fabrics had beautiful, natural curves from a torn edge or a random cut that had been accentuated by various dyeing, rinsing and ironing processes. On to these layered fabrics was placed a small fragment from my stored collection. It had a limited palette of limes, lemons and mustard yellows and was laid on an acid green background. A small area of soft turquoise and a dash of a strong marmalade orange fabric were then couched in place to enrich the colours.

The idea of using only straight stitches seemed to work well with the strong lines of the ribbed fabric and the applied fabrics. An area of fine, long, spidery stitches was taken across the dark maroon and chrome yellow to add a different rhythm and movement in the low, central area of the piece. The saturation of the colour is rich, uncompromising and boldly striking. Most of all, it was fun to do.

**Below:** Caught Vista 1, *the first in my series of townscapes.*

**Right:** *Detail showing running stitch and couching on a variety of different dyed fabrics.*

The second composition worked with a similar arrangement of elements, but I changed the colour proportions and the placement of the focal point. This slightly simpler composition was also worked from dark to light, keeping the main area of activity to a central piece with lines of fabric fragments and couched threads. This restrained central area consists of deep, rich orange, acid and lime green, and pale chalky and faded blue. I used mainly matt cottons, which look soft against the narrow slash of shiny bright green viscose satin; the contrast is powerful. This narrow band contrasts well with the magenta and purple rib underneath it and the deep indigo blue behind the stitching. It makes a striking composition: forceful and direct.

**Right:** Caught Vista 2.

**Below:** *Detail, showing the dyed fabric variations.*

The third composition became a stretched rectangular landscape. The piece was centred around a remnant: a tiny fragment of orange, magenta, yellow and pond-weed green fabrics. By laying these pieces on to a series of different reds, magentas and pinks, I created an impression of something distant but powerful. I wanted the elements to be small in a universe of colour, and in selecting the fabrics various natural curves began to become important. The gentle curve of shaded lilac violet laid on to a deep marigold yellow made a strong skyline and sandwiched the central area of colour by the use of a corn and ochre area at the bottom. Another central element was a piece of painted viscose satin that provided a reflection of more oranges and unexpected changes to a soft green.

Although these three pieces have a limited palette, there is a varied selection of colour and, on close inspection, little areas of the unexpected appear: a patch of blue, or is it mauve stitching? This is contrasted with a simple piece of shiny tarnished gold green fabric at the other end.

**Right:** Caught Vista 3, *showing the variety and quality of fabrics and techniques used. The complete piece is shown on pages 124–125.*

**Below:** *Detail of* Caught Vista 3, *showing the variety of hand stitching as well as the layering of transparent fabrics.*

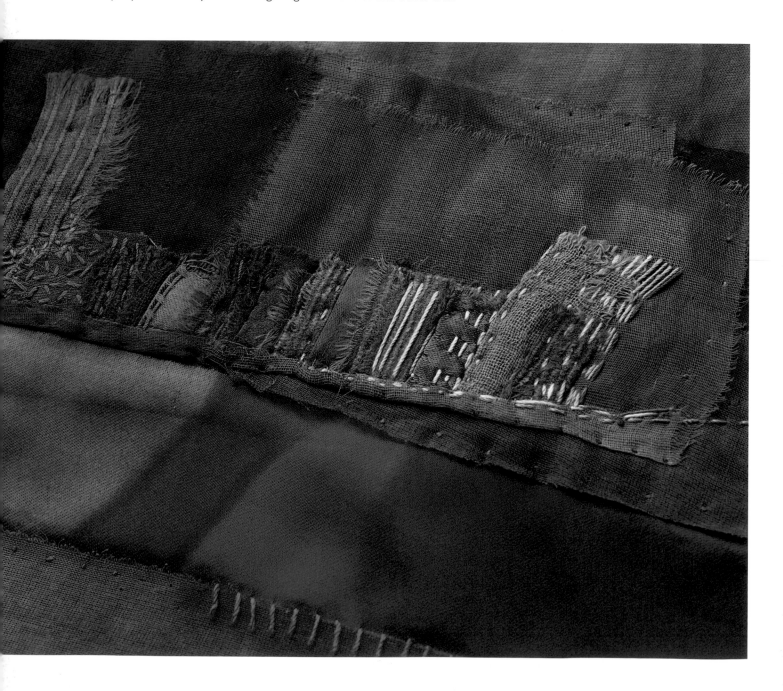

## Caught Vista 3

*A final exuberant statement offering
generous helpings of colour that
provide an impression of something
distant but powerful.*

# Index

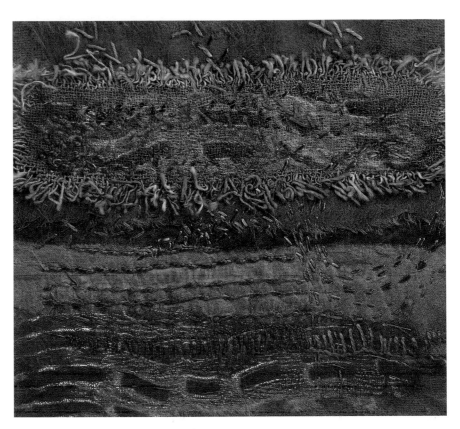

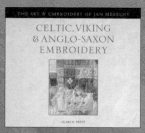
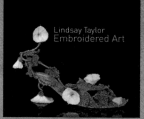

# A Passion for Colour

## Dedication

To Chas and our family, who always support me so much; to my colleagues, for all their encouragement; to all the students who enjoy being part of my 'research'; and finally to Katie and Roz, who have helped me get the words on to paper.